HOW TO FIND INFORMATION

•

PATENTS ON THE INTERNET

By DAVID NEWTON

THE BRITISH LIBRARY

Sponsored by

How to find information: patents on the Internet

ISBN 0-7123-0864-4

Published by:
The British Library
96 Euston Road
London NW1 2DB

British Library Cataloguing-in-Publication Data
A catalogue record is available for this book from the British Library

Desktop publishing by Concerto, Leighton Buzzard, Bedfordshire
Tel 01525 378757

Printed in Great Britain by Atheneum Press Ltd, Gateshead, Tyne and Wear

Further details about The British Library are available on its website:
http://www.bl.uk

Contents

Chapter 1.   Introduction

This small volume is intended to provide pointers to the information about patents that is available on the Internet. It does not aim to provide help in setting up or using the Internet per se although some information is given about special requirements for using particular patent services. No knowledge of patents or patent searching is assumed and some websites giving basic information on these topics are listed. It is possible to use the Web for searching to see if an invention is truly new but to have a high level of confidence in the results will require more experience of patents than this book alone can give. Nevertheless, a simple search using what is available for free on the Web may provide sufficient information if the purpose is to undertake a first screening of the invention.

The Internet grows at a tremendous speed and practically any organisation in the developed world of any size now has a Web presence. These organisations usually provide a wealth of up-to-date information on themselves and on their sphere of interest although this is sometimes advertising or 'soft' information rather than 'hard' data. Recently, many governments and inter-governmental organisations have been persuaded or cajoled to place on the Web huge volumes of commercially useful information and databases. This movement has included the national and international patent offices and in particular the European Patent Office, the United States Patent and Trademark Office, the Japanese Patent Office and the World Intellectual Property Organization have mounted huge patent databases. For example the United States Patent and Trademark Office database comprises 2.1 million patents and the European Patent Office Esp@cenet worldwide database consists of records of some 30 million patents and all this is available without charge. It must be said that there are deficiencies in these databases in that they do not allow the complex searching available in many commercial value-added databases such as those mentioned in Chapter 5. It should also be noted that although some databases include data for a number of earlier years a search in these sources does not necessarily go back as many years as is necessary for a comprehensive novelty search. A search, in any case, will depend on the skills of the searcher who needs to know the technology, the classification scheme, the terminology, the patent systems and so on.

Patent databases on the Web are often free but there are many value-added charged services which offer more extensive or superior data or greater ability to search. Both types are discussed in Chapters 4, 5 and 6 although a greater emphasis is placed in this book on the free services where newcomers to patent searching are more likely to start.

This text does not discuss the technology of the Internet but it is sufficient to distinguish between the main types of communication available over the Internet. These are:

- Firstly, the World Wide Web (generally known as the Web) which enables hyper-linking (using HTTP, Hypertext Transfer Protocol) so that by the click of a mouse you can view a further page of information from, possibly, a totally different location.

- Secondly, e-mail, which apart from being a method of sending correspondence, is a system by which you can join some discussion lists (or bulletin boards).

- Thirdly, FTP or File Transfer Protocol, which allows files to be transferred to and from remote computers.

- Fourthly, Telnet which allows you to log into a remote computer.

- Fifthly, newsgroups, which allow discussion of topics among Internet users.

This book will concentrate almost entirely on what is available on the World Wide Web.

To view Web pages requires a 'Browser' to be running on your PC. The two main versions of browser which are available are Netscape Navigator and Microsoft Internet Explorer. Some websites require you to use a recent version of this software so that the full facilities of the site can be used. These browsers can be downloaded without charge from **http://www.netscape.com/** and **http://www.microsoft.com/windows/ie/**. Some information that you may wish to view can require use of a helper or 'plug-in' to work with the browser, the most frequently encountered being Adobe Acrobat. Again this viewer software can be obtained without charge from the producer, in the case of Acrobat at the Adobe Web-site at **http://www.adobe.com/prodindex/acrobat/**. The United States Patent and Trademark Office has a Patent Full-Text Database (*see* page 16) which can be searched with standard software but if you want to view or print copies of the patent documents retrieved in the search this requires the loading of a plug-in viewer such as 'AlternaTIFF' free from Medical Informatics Engineering at **http://www.mieweb.com/alternatiff/**. In this case your PC has to be running a Windows 32-bit operating system such as Windows 95, 98 or NT. The Apple Macintosh will require different software. Some services work best with Java or JavaScript, which are normally available within your browser, but may need to be enabled within the browser preferences. Other services, such as the Australian databases, may require JavaScript to be enabled to operate at all.

The commonly used Web search engines, such as Alta Vista **http://www.altavista.com/**, Excite **http://www.excite.com/**, Go.com **http://infoseek.go.com/**, Google **http://www.google.com/**, Hotbot

http://hotbot.lycos.com/, and Northern Light http://www.
northernlight.com/ can be used to locate relevant information available over
the Web but these will not locate information within databases, such as those
listed in Chapters 4 and 5. A number of the major search engines offer directories
containing categorised lists of websites but the most useful of these for the topic
of intellectual property is Yahoo http://dir.yahoo.com/Government/Law/
Intellectual_Property/.

Not only is the Web doubling in size every year but the content is very large (a
recent estimate put the size of the Web as about 1,790 million pages) so that it is
difficult in a printed volume such as this for the references to be up-to-date at
the time of printing let alone by the time you come to read it. The solution to
this problem is the British Library's own patent pages on the Web. At our patent
site http://www.bl.uk/services/stb/patents.html you will find all the patent
links (see especially http://www.bl.uk/services/stb/etalmenu.html) noted
in this book with updates, replacements and new Web pages as they become
known to us. If you encounter an error when going to a new website it may be
worthwhile, after checking you have used the correct spellings, to enter the part
of the address as far as the last slash (/) and omit the last part as this may take you
to the 'parent' page on the same site.

In this book Web pages are referenced in bold as in the paragraph above. To
display the page in your browser you should enter the reference (known as an
URL or Uniform Resource Locator) exactly as shown but without any full stop
or closing bracket. The reference can be entered in the box labelled 'netsite' or
'location' in Netscape Navigator or 'address' in Microsoft Internet Explorer. Very
long addresses may have been split in this book where they are too long to fit on
a line but the reference should always be entered as a single line without spaces or
line breaks. In practice the first part of the references beginning http:// can be
omitted.

Chapter 2. The Patent System and Patenting

Although preparation may have begun before, the formal process for getting the grant of a patent begins with the submission of an application to the patent office. The patent office will generally search the application to check whether the invention meets all the criteria required by the law, including novelty. If allowed, the application will then be granted and published with any amendments demanded by the patent office. In many countries the procedure is for the patent office to publish the details of the patent application before it has been granted in addition to publishing them at grant. Once granted a patent will stay in force for 20 years from the original date of application subject to renewal or maintenance fees being paid by the owner. Thus the printed patent documents you see may be at any one of three stages; patent application not yet granted; a granted patent having legal status as a monopoly; or as an expired patent. In an initial search it may not be apparent which of these stages each patent application has reached.

Often the best place to look for information about taking out a patent is the relevant national patent office (*see* Appendix 2). Generally an inventor applies for a patent in their home country before considering applying for protection in foreign jurisdictions. The British Patent Office's website has information including: Frequently asked questions; How to prepare a UK patent application; Manual of Patent Practice; Use of academic papers to found a patent application; Assistance to inventors and help with your application; Fees; and International patent protection. Their website is at **http://www.patent.gov.uk/dpatents/ index.html**. The United States Patent and Trademark Office have similar information for the US system at **http://www.uspto.gov/web/menu/ pats.html**.

There are two International agreements to assist in getting protection in Europe and worldwide. These are the European Patent Convention (EPC) and the Patent Co-operation Treaty (PCT). In the former case the European Patent Office Applicants Guide is a good place to start at **http://www.european–patent– office.org/ap_gd/index.htm**. In the case of the PCT there are details at the World Intellectual Property Organization site at **http://www.wipo.int/eng/ mainpct.htm**.

The European Patent Convention covers most of the countries of Western Europe and some in Eastern Europe as well. In searching for all patents that are valid in any member country, such as the UK, it is important to search both for national patents and for European Patents that designate (and take effect in) the UK.

Most inventors and inventing companies employ patent agents (attorneys) to prosecute their patent applications and generally to look after their intellectual property rights. Information about patenting and about the services of British Patent Agents is given at the Chartered Institute of Patent Agents site at **http://www.cipa.org.uk/**. Corresponding information for the US is given on the American Intellectual Property Law Association site at **http://www.aipla. org/**. Names of European patent lawyers, many of which are also British patent agents, can be searched at **http://www.european-patent-office.org/reps/ search.html** and further details about their organisation, the European Patent Institute, can be found at **www.patentepi.com/english/index.html**. PatentPro at **http://www.4patpro.com/** is software which takes information on an invention and creates an application for a US patent without the necessity of employing a patent attorney but the author has not seen it in operation.

The main hurdle to getting the grant of a patent is novelty. That is, an invention must not have been disclosed anywhere in the world in a published patent application, in a journal or in any other published document, at an exhibition or conference or, if a product, have been sold to the public. If it has been disclosed before a patent application has been filed, except in certain circumstances in countries such as the US, a valid patent will not be granted. A 'novelty search' is carried out to test if an invention is novel. Once granted only the patent owner (or others with the owner's permission) are allowed to use, make or sell the invention in the countries where the patent is in force. To avoid flouting other people's patents, manufacturers and traders may need to run an 'infringement search' to obtain clearance. This kind of search asks the question, 'what valid patents currently in force embrace the technology I intend to use?' Novelty and infringement searches are two flavours of patent subject searches.

Utility models are a form of intellectual property rights available in some countries like patents but having a lower level of inventiveness and a shorter term of protection. Utility models may need to be covered in a patent search but not all databases include them. Utility models, sometimes known as petty patents or Gebrauchsmustern in German, should not be confused with 'utility patents', a term sometimes used to describe regular patents in the US.

New plant varieties can be protected by a separate right (*see* **http://www.upov. org/eng/index.htm**) and a separate provision exists in the US for plant patents (*see* **http://www.uspto.gov/web/offices/pac/plant/index.html**).

Registered designs, or design patents, are another form of intellectual property rights which protect the appearance of an object rather than its function. Designs are not covered in this book except incidentally. Trade marks, which are used to distinguish goods and services, and copyright, which is used to protect literary and artistic works, are also forms of intellectual property rights that are not covered.

Chapter 3.   The Patent Subject Search

Since over 40 million patents have been issued across the world searching for any subject can be complex. To help themselves and you search, the patent offices have devised classification schemes which are particularly good at assisting in searches for novelty, that is answering the question, 'has my invention been previously invented and disclosed by someone else?' The aim of the classification scheme is to divide up the subject matter into areas containing a small number of pertinent documents which can then be manually scanned for relevance. If the aim of the search is to determine the 'state of the art' in a subject area rather than just novelty then the patent classification may not be so helpful particularly if you are interested in an application or use and the classification categorises the subject by function. If classification is not suitable then keyword searching (*see* below), or a combination of the two, may be more appropriate.

Practically all patents over recent years have been classified by the issuing patent office using the International Patent Classification (IPC) and so this is a powerful method of universal subject searching. The IPC started in 1970 and has been revised regularly with a new edition being issued every five years. The 6th edition became operational at the beginning of 1995 and the 7th on 1 January 2000. To search documents issued over a number of years it will be necessary to check not only the 7th edition of the classification for the subject matter but also the corresponding classification in earlier editions of the IPC.

To find the correct IPC class start with the alphabetical index to the 7th edition (The Catchword Index linked from the page at **http://classifications. wipo.int/fulltext/new_ipc/index.htm**) while noting that although the IPC itself covers all subject-matter not all useful terms are listed in the index. The word you have looked up should lead to one or more places in the classification schedules and give you terms of the format 'G01W 1/04', where the first part, the subclass e.g. 'G01W', is given at the head of the page. The terms consist of a subclass symbol followed by two numbers each of one, two or three digits separated by an oblique stroke. Note that though this format is used on printed patent documents many databases reformat the IPC class, for example by removing the space or slash (/) or by making up the numbers following the subclass to three digits with leading zeros. Careful editing may be required when searching. Inventions too general to be classified at the finest level will be classified to a general (00) group e.g. 'G01W 1/00'.

You should read any relevant notes in the IPC schedule you are using and follow hyper-linked cross-references to arrive at the appropriate classification. Remember that each entry in the IPC schedules should be read together with successive higher levels until the whole classification is found. The various levels are shown by dots preceding the text e.g. a three dot entry (...Alternating ploughs) should be read in conjunction with the next highest two dot entry (.. with three or more wheels, or endless tracks), the next highest one dot entry (. Self propelled ploughs) and the group heading (Ploughs with fixed plough-shares). It is usually wise to search a broader range of classes than is strictly necessary. This is done by truncating the terms, e.g. by searching 'G01W' or 'G01W 1' rather than 'G01W 1/16', and then by subsequently defining the results found more narrowly as required. There are links on the World Intellectual Property Organization IPC page to 'Help' (about using the online IPC) and to a 'Guide' (giving further detail of how the IPC operates).

The European Patent Office uses the ECLA, European classification, in its Esp@cenet database as well as the IPC. ECLA is based on the IPC but is more detailed and is applied very consistently. What is more, the European Patent Office reclassifies its database as ECLA codes are updated. The definitions of ECLA are at **http://l2.espacenet.com/espacenet/ecla/index/index.htm**.

US patent documents are searchable by the US patent classification. As with ECLA, US patent documents are reclassified every time the US classification scheme is updated. A detailed alphabetical index to the classification is given at **http://www.patentec.com/data/class/Classes.html**. This leads to the detailed Manual of Classification. The United States Patent and Trademark Office has its own classification information at **http://www.uspto.gov/go/taf/moc/index.htm**. The button 'Classification definitions' leads to the alphabetical list of terms used in the classification and following the hyper-links shown will lead to the full class and subclass text. An alternative, possibly more convenient, is the classes and subclasses listing found in the classification schedules at the IBM Intellectual Property Network site at **http://www.patents.ibm.com/patlist?xcl=0**. By starting with a generic term it allows you to work down the hierarchy to arrive at the final code and a list of documents bearing this classification. The USA patent classification is widely searchable in the United States Patent and Trademark Office, IBM, MicroPatent, QPAT, Community of Science, PatIntelligence and many other US patent databases. A concordance from the US patent classification to the IPC (but not the other way around) is at **http://www.uspto.gov/web/offices/ac/ido/oeip/taf/ipc_conc/index.html** but it should not be relied upon as a method of finding the correct IPC for a topic.

Often an easier way of finding the correct classification is to look at the way one or more particularly relevant patent documents have been classified and then to search using that classification. However, this method should not be the only approach for a thorough search.

The Derwent World Patents Index database (*see* page 25) uses, as well as the IPC, its own classification and indexing schemes which may allow better retrieval in many cases. The Claims database (*see* page 25) also has its own chemical indexing. Chemical Abstracts and some other subject based services which include patents also have their own indexing schemes but these databases are not covered in this book.

Keyword searching can be used in databases as an alternative to classification searching or as an adjunct to it. It is particularly useful where the classification systems do not well match the concepts to be searched. However, you may not be able to locate relevant patents because the words that have been used in the documents you need to find may not be the ones you would think of searching; they may be synonyms or be broader concepts or alternative descriptions. You will need to create a search strategy that includes all the terms which can be used to describe the concept to be searched. A thesaurus or technical dictionary might be useful in obtaining synonyms for this purpose. See for example the Web of online dictionaries at **http://www.facstaff.bucknell.edu/rbeard/ diction5.html**. Wherever possible you will need to use 'truncation' of the search terms so as to include plurals and other endings and to include US- and UK-English spellings. Some databases may automatically provide 'stemming' which will pick up all forms of a word with the same stem but otherwise truncation is required. It is usually better to use lower case rather than capitals as in searching with the latter some systems will only find words that have been capitalised whereas lower case will find both.

You may be used to Web searching in which the search engine will respond to a query with results containing any of the requested words but listing the most relevant hits first. Patent searching on the Web usually uses strict Boolean logic; that is if you search for 'word A' AND 'word B' the result set will include only those patents having both words present whereas searching for 'word A' OR 'word B' will result in a list of patents with either word present. See the entries in Appendix 1 for further information on Boolean logic and operators. The order in which the results are displayed is often the most recent first but some databases use relevance ranking based on frequency of occurrence of selected terms and others may allow the user to select the order.

Word searching can often be carried out in the title, the abstract or the full text of the patent. Searching just the title may not find all the relevant material whereas searching the full text may give too many results and in some cases give results where the keywords have appeared in the 'prior art' section of the document. It may be possible to search just the claims, the part that defines the monopoly of the patent. If some of the patents are not in the English-language this will present further problems for searching.

The best search strategy might be to search using a broad (truncated) classification symbol to limit the patents to a particular technology AND some keywords to define the area of interest. e.g. pens for writing are in class B43 of the IPC but pens for animals and so on are elsewhere so a search using 'B43 AND cleaning' and so on might be superior to a search using the words 'pen' or 'pens' to find 'ball point pens with integral cleaning mechanisms'.

To verify whether an invention is novel requires not only searching of the patent literature but, strictly, a search of all other published literature. The necessity for this will depend on the subject-matter and the level of comprehensiveness required. The World Intellectual Property Organization have produced JOPAL (*Journal of Patent Associated Literature*) to assist in searching over 200 key scientific and technical journals. The Web database **http://jopal.wipo.int/** provides access to JOPAL data from 1981 and can be searched by title words or by the IPC. A useful patent-like source is *IBM Technical Disclosure Bulletin*. This periodical contains disclosures published between 1958 and January 1998, mainly from research by IBM staff, which have not been patented. The periodical is searchable by keyword, or can be browsed through by issue at **http://www.patents.ibm.com/tdb**. Information on more general literature searching is outside the scope of this book.

Chapter 4.   Key Search Databases

This chapter gives some detail of a few of the most useful sources for patent searching with emphasis on those that are available without charge or registration. At the foot of each 'key facts' table a rating is given of some of the features. The more stars given the higher the opinion of that feature. This is inevitably a subjective assessment and will not be a universally useful indication of the use of a database for a particular purpose.

Esp@cenet

Esp@cenet – key facts

URLs:	**http://gb.espacenet.com** or **http://ep.espacenet.com**
Produced by:	European Patent Office

Coverage:

22 different databases
1. Worldwide 30 million patents including US, GB, CH, DE, FR, SE from 1920, EP, WO from 1978. (*See* Appendix 3 for further details of coverage).
2. European Patents 1997-date
3. Patent Co-operation Treaty applications 1997-date; (The same data is also available on the Patent Co-operation Treaty Gazette database – *see* page 19.)
4   Japanese patent abstracts in English (PAJ) 1976-. Generally 6 months behind publication in Japanese. For other versions of PAJ *see* Chapter 6.
5. British patent applications 06/1996 to date
6 to 22. Other European countries AT 1995-, BE 1996-, CH 1994-, CY 1995-, DE 1997-, DK 06/1996-05/1998, ES 1996-, FI- 1994, FR 1997-, GR 11/1997-, IE 06/1996- 12/1997, IT 1997-, LU 1998-, MC 1996-, NL 05/1994-, PT 1997-, SE 1970-.

Search:

Ten Fields in the Worldwide database (less in the other databases) - *see* Figure 1. No index browsing; no cross links from citations; no proximity searching possible.

Title:
Acetic acid will retrieve patents with these two words anywhere in the title whereas "acetic acid" in quotation marks will find only occurrences where they appear as the exact phrase. The language of databases 6–22 is that of the original publication. Truncation is shortly to be made available.

Title and abstract:

As for title but more records will be found. Truncation is shortly to be made available.

Application Number:

Country code then year then seven digit number; can be truncated to country code e.g. GB. Application date can be searched e.g. 19950520 or the combination of country AND date e.g. GB AND 19970520 can be entered.

Priority Number:

Format is same as application number: Can be truncated to country code e.g. GB. Dates can be searched as for publication date.

Publication Date:

can be truncated to year e.g. 1997 or month, e.g. 199701, or input in full, e.g. 19970102.

Applicant:

Name of company or individual. Truncation currently not allowed. Common words e.g. international may be abbreviated and therefore not found in a search for the full term.

Inventor:

Note no truncation allowed e.g. A Smith will not find Alan Smith. But A Smith will find Smith J and Jones A as co-inventors.

EC Classification:

Based on the IPC but with additional subdivisions. ECLA is applied by the European Patent Office patent examiners. Format is identical to IPC but with additional letters and numbers after the IPC code.

IPC Classification:

Spaces must be eliminated from the classification symbol. Can be truncated to any level e.g. A01B 1/00 can be searched as can any of A or A01 or A01B or A01B1.

Viewing and Printing:

A list of the first 20 results is given with publication number and title. Further batches of 20 results can be viewed via the jump bar above the results list but no more than 500 results can be retrieved in any search. Clicking on an individual patent number gives more details which vary from names, dates and classification through title and abstract to images of the drawing, an abstract, title, and full text of the specification.

Content ★★★★★ Searching ★★   Viewing and printing ★★   Help ★

How to use Esp@cenet

This is the search system of the European Patent Office and can be accessed through any of the European national patent offices websites or direct via the European Patent Office or European Commission's IPR Help Desk. The language on the opening screens and help pages will be the language of the patent office through which you connected to Esp@cenet but the databases are identical however they are accessed. 22 databases are available: one for each member country of the European Patent Convention containing the recently published patent specifications; one for the recent European Patent Office applications; one for recent Patent Co-operation Treaty material; one for Japan; and, the most powerful, the worldwide database. The home page offers you a simple search screen which allows only text, patent number or applicant name searching in the worldwide database but it also offers the choice of selecting from any of the databases. Clicking on any one database link takes you to the main search screen (Figure 1) which always has a similar format. Connecting through the European Patent Office or the IPR Help Desk websites does not allow use of any of the national databases (except Japan) whereas access through any of the national offices allows use of any of the databases.

On the left of the main search screen (Figure 1) are eight icons which appear, so long as the function is available, as raised buttons when the mouse is passed over them. These icons are Home (house icon), Search (binoculars), Results list (text without image icon), Document viewer (a page with an image), Shopping basket (shopping cart), Help (?), Information and news (i), and Feedback (envelope). On this screen you can enter the words or details you wish to search. After clicking the search button you are taken to the Results list page (Figure 2) where the numbers and titles of the patents found are listed. The bibliographic details of the listed patents can be viewed in turn on the document viewer screen (Figure 3) by clicking on the patent numbers. To view the details of the next or another listed patent you first go back to the Results list screen and then to another patent in the list. The document viewer screen gives bibliographic details such as patent number and title and in some cases an abstract. Above the bibliographic information are some buttons which show what other details are available, for example a drawing and claims page. It may be necessary to scroll to the right to see all of the buttons. By clicking on the patent numbers given (Requested Patent or Equivalents) an image of the front page of the patent specification will be fetched and further buttons will then allow specific pages to be retrieved e.g. the next or previous pages or the first page of the description or search report (S.R.). By moving through the pages in this way the whole patent document can be seen and printed out, if required. The pages of the patent document are delivered as PDF files and the Adobe Acrobat reader has to be installed to view them (*see* page 2).

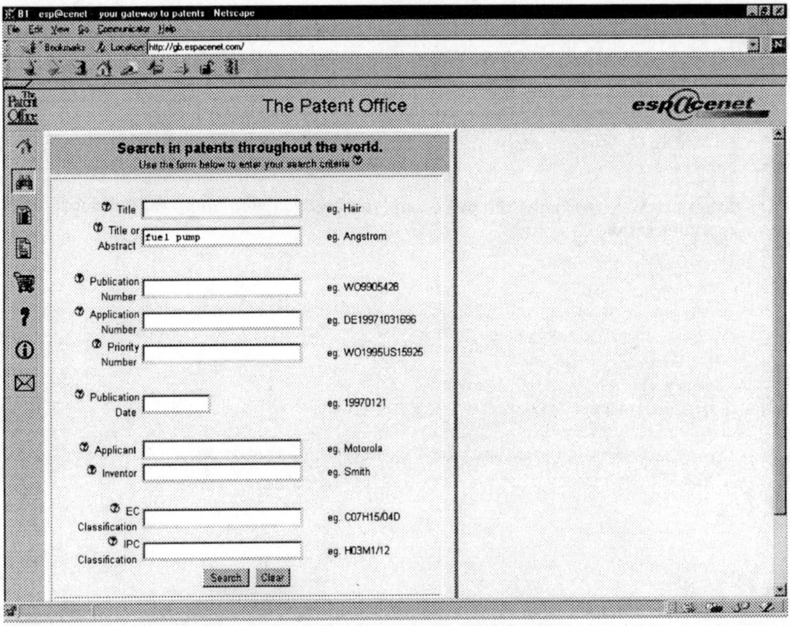

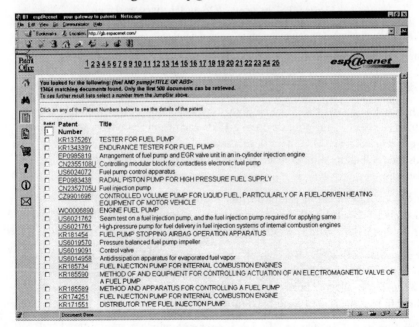

Figure 1 Esp@cenet Search screen

Figure 2 Esp@cenet Result lists page

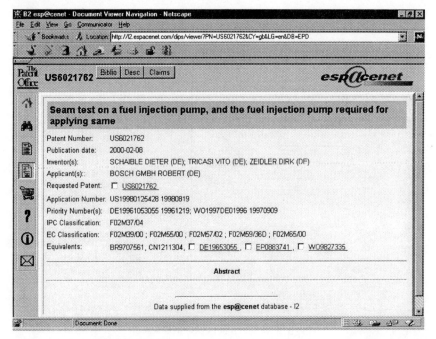

Figure 3 Esp@cenet Document viewer screen

In this process three windows will be opened (these may be seen as buttons on the task bar in Windows 95/98/NT). They are labelled B1 for the Search screen and Results list; B2 for the document viewer; and B3 for the Document pages. Using the buttons for these pages can make it easier to navigate back and forth.

The worldwide database is a comprehensive collection of patents published since 1920. For documents published since 1970, each patent family in the collection has a representative document with a searchable English-language title and abstract. Appendix 3 gives further detail of the coverage of the worldwide database.

If you require copies of patent documents, of which you know the numbers, it is possible to download all the document pages in one go from Esp@cenet by use of the Lattice software (*see* page 41).

It is possible to use the Boolean operators 'OR', 'AND' and 'NOT' within a field to link synonyms, to limit terms or to exclude records. Right-hand truncation is not currently allowed but is planned. The search terms you enter in the boxes for the different fields are linked by an implied 'AND'.

The European Classification, ECLA, is a scheme which is administered and applied by the European Patent Office, so it has the benefit of the consistency from use by a single organisation. The classification is automatically updated as new or modified codes are introduced.

The help available is quite extensive but the European Commission's IPR Help Desk have introduced a tutorial covering Esp@cenet at **http://www.ipr-helpdesk.org/mm/esptut/index.htm**. Under the heading 'Basics' the tutorial discusses patents and patenting in general and under 'Essentials' and 'Step by step' provides information on Esp@cenet itself.

United States Patent and Trade Mark Office

USPTO Web Patent Databases – key facts

URL:	http://www.uspto.gov/patft/index.html
Produced by:	United States Patent and Trademark Office

Coverage:
Two separate databases, the Patent Full-Text Database and The Patent Bibliographic Database, both covering United States patents including utility patents, design patents, plant patents, reissues, defensive publications and Statutory Invention Registrations. These databases cover the period from 1 January 1976 (patent no. 3930271) to the most recent weekly issue date (usually each Tuesday). The Full-Text database allows searching of the complete text of the patent specifications but the Bibliographic Database is faster to search. Images of the complete patent documents are available from 1976.

Search:
The simplest option is the *Patent Number Search* which enables searching for a known patent number. Clicking on the patent number and title found in this search will result in a display of the relevant bibliographic information but not the full text of the patent specifications or the facsimile image of the patent itself.

Apart from the above option The Patent Full-Text Database and The Patent Bibliographic Database both have two search screens: the Boolean Search Page and the Manual (or Advanced) Search Page.

The Boolean Search Page is the simplest option and it allows a date range to be specified along with one or two keywords or other terms. It works in a similar way in both Full text and Bibliographic databases. A single word or term can be entered in Term 1 box and qualified with a field descriptor. This term can then be combined, if required, with a second term in the TERM 2 box using 'AND' (to restrict the search), or 'OR' (to enlarge the search) or 'ANDNOT' (to eliminate patents containing the second term). *See* Figure 4.

The Manual (or Advanced) Search Page again allows a date range to be selected and complex statements to be searched using Boolean logic. Each term can be qualified using a field code (listed below) and if not qualified it will apply across all fields. Truncation of terms is allowed and the symbol $ is used in the Full-text database whereas * is used in a Bibliographic search.

Viewing and printing:
Clicking the Search button in the Patent Full-Text Database or the Patent Bibliographic Database results in a list of up to 50 patent numbers and titles.

Further batches of 50 hits can be obtained by clicking the Next 50 Hits button. Clicking on any of the patents listed will result in the display of the full text of the specification including bibliographic information or just the bibliographic details according to whether the Full text or Bibliographic databases are being searched.

Facsimiles of the pages of the patent document can be retrieved by clicking on the Images button in the Full Text database provided the correct viewing software is loaded (*see* page 2). Citations can be followed.

Content ** Searching ** Viewing and printing * Help ****

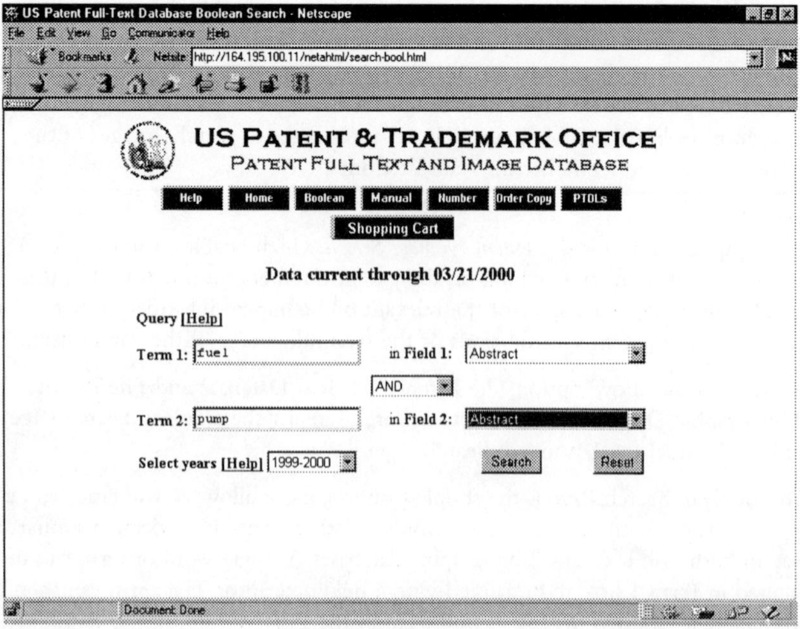

Figure 4 United States Patent and Trademark Office Boolean search screen

Fields used in the United States Patent and Trademark Office database

Application Date	APD	Inventor City	IC
Abstract	ABST	Inventor Country	ICN
Application Serial Number	APN	Inventor Name	IN
Application Type	APT	Inventor State	IS
Assignee City	AC	Issue Date	ISD
Assignee Country	ACN	Other References	OREF
Assignee Name	AN	Parent Case Information	PARN
Assignee State	AS	Patent Number	PN
Assistant Examiner	EXA	PCT Information	PCT
Attorney or Agent	LREP	Primary Examiner	EXP
Claims	ACLM	Reissue Data	REIS
Description/Specification	SPEC	Title	TTL
Foreign Priority	PRIR	Related US Application Data	RLAP
Foreign References	FREF	Issued US Classification	CLAS
Government Interest	GOVT	US References	REF
International Classification	ICL		

IBM Intellectual Property Network

Intellectual Property Network – key facts

URL:	**http://www.patents.ibm.com/home**
Produced by:	International Business Machines. Free of charge but the subscription IPN for business database offers additional features.

Coverage:
US Text/Database from 05 January 1971
US Images from 01 January 1974
EP A documents. Text/Database/Images from 10 January 1979

EP B documents. Title text/Database/Images from 9 January 1980

PCT Text/Database from 01 January 1990; Images from 01 January 1990

JP Database in English (PAJ) and images (first page only) from October 1976. For other versions of PAJ *see* Chapter 6.

Inpadoc. Worldwide database from 1968 (*see* page 29).

Not so current as Esp@cenet for EP and PCT.

Search:

The search is conducted in the title and abstract text (or title only in the case of the EP documents) with the option of searching the claims of the US patents. The system uses automatic stemming (e.g. 'devices' is truncated to 'device', 'asserting' to 'assert') and this occurs in all text fields including names but it can be turned off by using the 'WORD' operator. Proximity operators 'NEAR'. 'PARAGRAPH', etc. can be used (*see* the Search Language description page **http://patent.womplex.ibm.com/langhelp**)

Four types of search are available: Simple text, Patent number, Boolean text and Advanced text. The Simple Text Search on the homepage is used to find patents containing a specific word or phrase. The Boolean Text Search allows up to four boxes to be filled in with keywords or data from various fields. These can be tagged with specified fields and linked with the Boolean operators 'AND', 'OR', 'AND NOT'. The Advanced Text search page is similar but provides boxes for each field. Keywords and other data entered into these fields are combined with the 'AND' operator. The Patent Number search allows just a number search.

Viewing and printing:

Clicking on the search button gives a results list consisting of patent number, issue date and title. Clicking on the document number gives the front page data for the patent including related US patents, US claims, references to other patents and literature and references to the patent by later patents. Family data are also given and the Inpadoc database provides legal status data. Citations of US patents can be followed. The full document can be viewed by clicking on view image (or on the thumb nail image). Patents are retrieved page by page but printing from these does not generally produce a good result. Documents can be ordered for downloading as PDF or TIFF files for a fee.

Content ★★★★   Searching ★★★   Viewing and printing ★★   Help ★★★★

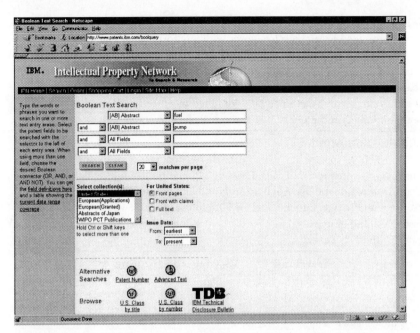

Figure 5 IBM Intellectual Property Network Boolean Text Search page

Patent Co-operation Treaty Gazette

Patent Co-operation Treaty Gazette – key facts

URL: **http://pctgazette.wipo.int/**

Produced by: World Intellectual Property Organization

Coverage:
Contains the first page data (bibliographic data, English-language abstract and drawing) of published PCT applications (WO) from 1.1.1997 (same data as Esp@cenet database 4 – *see* above).

Search:
There are two options – Search and Browse. Browse allows the viewing of all or a selection by IPC of the patent applications issued in one week. Use Search for searching the entire database. Queries may be entered as keywords or terms (qualified, if required, by Field Codes such as ABE for keyword in the English-language abstract), Boolean operators ('AND', 'OR', 'ANDNOT', 'XOR') can be used to search complex topics and the proximity operator 'NEAR' can be used to

19

search for terms within 20 characters of one another. Right truncation using the ★ operator allows searching for words with any form of ending. In a search using the patent classification IPCs should be entered in the style H03F-3/45, for example. For users who create an account (no charge), a history of the last 20 searches conducted is kept. The results can be recalled at a later time and also the search strategy can be subsequently modified by entering $Rn, where n is the search number, in the query box along with further search statements.

Viewing and printing:

It is possible to specify the elements of the records you wish to display by checking the appropriate boxes. These are: Publication Number, Title, Publication Date, International Class, Application Number, First Inventor, First Applicant, Abstract and Image. Either 10, 25 or 50 results can be viewed at one go making fast skimming quite easy. The text of the documents (images) are available though links to the Esp@cenet site.

Content ★   Searching ★★★   Viewing and printing ★★★   Help ★★

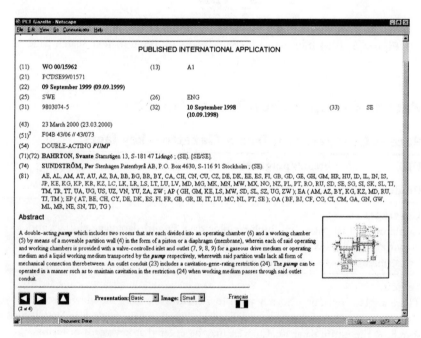

Figure 6 Patent Co-operation Treaty Gazette

PATON – Patentinformationszentrum und Online-Dienste

GlobalPat – key facts

URL: http://athena.patent-inf.tu-ilmenau.de/

Available from: TU Ilmenau / PATON (Patentinformationszentrum und Online-Dienste) from the GlobalPat database produced by the European Patent Office and the US Patent and Trademark Office. Now subscription only.

Coverage:

Bibliographic data and abstracts in English of the following: European Patent applications (EP), Patent Co-operation Treaty (WO), Germany (DE), France (FR), United Kingdom (GB), Switzerland (CH) and USA (US) from 1971. The database is, at the time of writing (June 2000), many months out of date. Database content: 3 million documents. If GlobalPat is searched with Patents Abstracts of Japan (PAJ) good world-wide coverage can be achieved. PATON also offers PAJ from 1976 and Patent Abstracts of Russia which are English summaries of Russian patent applications and patents from 1994 (*see* also Chapter 6 for other versions).

Search:

There are two search masks (English and German versions) allowing the following fields to be searched: Patent number, International Patent Classification (format e.g.H01H033-66), English title, Abstract, Patent applicant, Inventor, and 'Words anywhere'. Truncation can be used and the symbol is $ for any number of characters. Boolean operators and comprehensive adjacency operators are available. The 'Words anywhere' field can be used for entering any data from the above fields or additionally from many other fields such as dates and classification. Dates, e.g. priority, can be entered as @PRD=19870629. Different components of the IPC including the index terms can be searched (e.g. the IPC assigned as the main class as (E01H005-04).ICM or the IPC as assigned by the European Patent Office as (E01H005-04).ICE). A record is kept of the search history (back references) and earlier searches can be retraced and refined, if required.

Viewing and printing:

Hitting the search button at the bottom of the search mask brings up a list of patent numbers with English-language titles and sometimes a drawing. Clicking on the patent numbers takes you to the bibliographic information and abstract and also lists members of the patent family. Clicking on the icon next to the IPC symbol brings up the text of the relevant class. A further 'graph' icon will allow you to view a tabulated time series for one or more IPC symbols giving number of patents published each year.

Content ★★★   **Searching ★★**   **Viewing and printing ★★**   **Help ★**

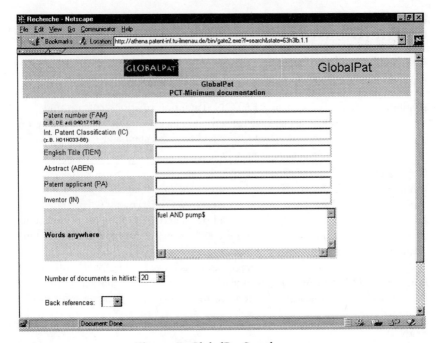

Figure 7 GlobalPat Search screen

Chapter 5.   Commercial Services and Value-Added Databases

At the foot of some of some of the Key facts tables ratings are given. *See* page 10 for notes on this topic.

QPAT

QPAT*WW – key facts

URL:	http://www.qpat.com
Produced by:	Questel–Orbit. Subscription service with monthly and annual rates. Free search of abstracts.

Coverage:
Full text of US patents since 1 Jan 1974, EP-A since 1987 and EP-B since 1991. It is intended to include WO during 2000. Images of all patents are displayable.

Search:
Two types of search are available: Field Search and Standard Search.

The Field Search allows words or other terms to be entered in boxes (qualified as required by one of up to 40 fields) and then linked by Boolean logic to other boxes containing words or terms.

The Standard Search provides a screen area for entering a search expression in which words or terms can be flexibly linked and qualified (using any of the fields).

In either type of search, terms can be truncated (? or *) and various forms of adjacency operators are available. Automatic stemming, in which all the various endings of a word are searched with the specified word, is available.

IPC classification is entered as e.g. (A01B-035-0026)/ic or (A01B)/ic or (A01B-035)/ic. If required, the edition of the IPC can be specified.
A panel on the left of the screen allows the US and/or EP databases to be searched and the date (publication or priority) range to be specified.
Citations of US patents can be followed.

Viewing and Printing:
Hitting the search button reveals the number of results from the search and a recap of the search strategy appears in the lower right-hand section of the screen

along with a Search ID number. These details are maintained throughout the search session and any search strategy can be modified by incorporating the search ID number in subsequent searches. Clicking on the Search ID gives a list of patent numbers (the first 25 to 300) and titles (these can be ordered by relevance, title, date, country or patent number) and an Expanded View option displays patent number, title and the first two lines of the abstract. Further details (abstracts or full text) of individual patents can be brought to the screen by clicking on the patent number or, usefully, by checking the required patents on the list all of them can be brought to the screen in one go.

The results in the frame can be printed.

Content ★★   Searching ★★★★ Viewing and printing ★★★★   Help ★★

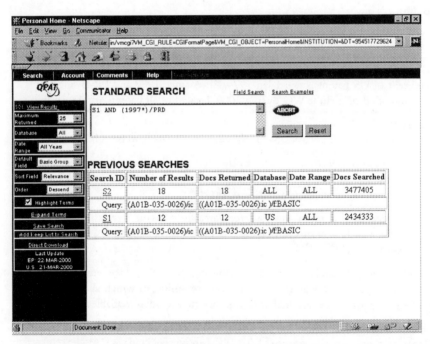

Figure 8 QPAT standard search screen

World Patents Index

WPI – key facts

Produced by: Derwent Information (**http://www.derwent.com**).
Subscription service available through hosts:
Questel-Orbit at **http://www.questel.orbit.com/**,
Dialog at **http://www.dialogweb.com/** and
STN at **http://stnweb.fiz-karlsruhe.de/** or
http://www.cas.org/stn.html.

Derwent now also offers the Derwent database as DII (Derwent Innovations Index) only on the Web. It offers the same basic data but with more limited search possibilities. Annual subscription.

Coverage:
Over 40 patenting authorities including US, EP, WO. 100% Japanese coverage from 1996. Covers pharmaceutical patents from 1963, agricultural and veterinary medicine from 1965, plastics and polymers from 1966, all chemistry from 1970, electronics, electrical and mechanical engineering from 1974. Comprehensive coverage of all technologies from 1974. Timeliness is two to ten weeks from issue date, for major patent-issuing authorities.

Search:
DWPI contains a wealth of information and is searched most flexibly using a host command language. The hosts each have different interfaces. Each DWPI record represents a patented invention and if patents for an invention have been filed in more than one patent office, all of the patent publication details are combined into a single record. All records contain patent family information. Searching is in English-language abstracts and enhanced titles. Value-added structural chemistry and other indexing can also be searched. DII allows citations to be followed.

Viewing and printing:
The options are extremely flexible. Abstracts, bibliographic and family information can be viewed and patent drawings are available for patents since 1988.

WPI **Content ★★★★★ Searching ★★ Viewing and printing ★★★ Help ★★**
DII **Content ★★★★★ Searching ★★★ Viewing and printing ★★★ Help ★★★★**

MicroPatent

MicroPatent Web Patent Databases – key facts

URL: http://www.micropat.com

Produced by: MicroPatent. Subscription service with daily and annual rates.

Coverage:

Two separate databases: Worldwide PatSearch and PatSearch FullText. These databases cover US, EP and Patent Co-operation Treaty patent specifications and Japanese English-language abstracts (PAJ) from 1 January 1976 but the FullText database contains EP documents only from 1988 and WO from 1983. *See* Chapter 6 for other versions of PAJ.

Search:

The simplest options are on the Worldwide PatSearch screen. First, Search by Number which enables searching for a known patent number. Second, a Simple Search allows you to enter keywords for search in titles, abstracts, inventors and assignees/applicants in a single line. The Fielded Search allows more complex searches by keywords and other terms to be entered into a form and linked using Boolean logic. It is also possible to specify that terms must be adjacent ('ADJ' and 'NEAR' operators) and to truncate the terms (* is a wild card to represent any number of characters and ? is used to represent a single character). Clicking the Search button on the search screen allows a list of 25 to 500 patent numbers and titles to be displayed. Further batches of hits can be obtained by clicking the Next button.

The PatSearch FullText allows the complete text of the patent specifications to be searched (or parts of the text such as the claims). Keywords in the specification can be searched using the same Boolean operators as above. The operators 'WITH' and 'SAME' can also be used to specify that keywords must be in the same sentence or paragraph respectively. The results of a keyword search can be limited by specifying terms that must be present in other fields. The hitlist can be sorted according to issue date, class or applicant/assignee name. A history of searches previously carried out is available.

Viewing and printing:

Clicking on any of the patents listed will result in the display of the front page data or full text (including formulae and drawings) of the specification according to whether the PatSearch FullText or Worldwide PatSearch databases are being searched. From the bibliographic page a list of the patent family members can be obtained. Citations of US patents can be followed.

Clicking on the download button for any patent (on the FullText page) allows you to view the front page of the patent. This can be viewed using the MicroPatent® PatentImage Viewer, a multi-page TIFF viewer, or Adobe® Acrobat reader for PDF files (*see* page 2 for information on viewers). Previews are free if you order the corresponding patents within 24 hours. Otherwise there is a charge of $1.50 per preview. Various charged options are available for downloading the full patent or front page or for otherwise getting a copy of the document. Downloading is very rapid.

Content ★★★　　Searching ★★　　Viewing and printing ★★　　Help ★★

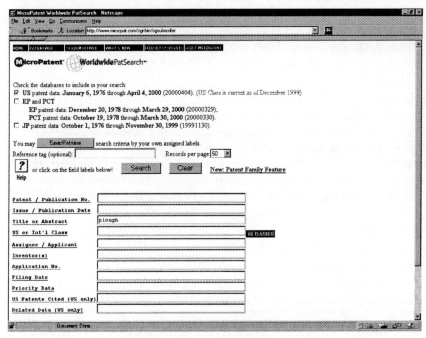

Figure 9 MicroPatent Worldwide PatSearch fielded search screen

CLAIMS/U.S. Patents Database

CLAIMS – key facts

Produced by: IFI Claims (**http://www.ificlaims.com/**).
Subscription service available through hosts:
Questel-Orbit at **http://www.questel.orbit.com/**,
Dialog at **http://www.dialogweb.com/** and
STN at **http://stnweb.fiz-karlsruhe.de/** or
http://www.cas.org/stn.html

Coverage:
The CLAIMS/U.S. Patents file covers all chemical and chemically related patents from 1950 to the present, and mechanical and electrical patents from 1963 to the present. Design patents and plant patents are covered from December 1976 to the present. A number of related databases are available. IFI updates the database weekly, providing online access to patent references within one week after issue of the patent.

Search:
CLAIMS contains detailed information and is best searched using a host command language. The hosts each have different interfaces. Searchable fields include the patent number and title, inventor and assignee names, and USPTO and IPC classifications. The file contains the broad claim for chemical patents from 1950 and for mechanical and electrical patents from 1963 to the present. Starting in 1971, the abstract is included for patents in all technologies. Also included from 1971 forward is front page information and other claims. Related files contain citation indexing and special in-depth subject indexes for chemical and chemically related patent searching.

Viewing and printing:
The options are extremely flexible and depend on the host system used. Searchable information is also viewable.

Content * Searching ** Viewing and printing ** Help ****

Manning and Napier PatentMiner

PatentMiner – key facts

URL:	**http://www.mnis.net/**
Produced by:	Manning and Napier. Subscription service with free searching of title and other bibliographic data.

Content:
Full text and bibliographic details of US patents since 1974.

Searching:
Searches in the bibliographic data and title are free and provide flexible truncation using the * symbol. A preview button allows browsing in the index to find near matches. For a more powerful search the natural language Concept Search can be used in conjunction with the bibliographic data filter. Relevancy can be adjusted by altering the importance of found words and phrases. US patent citations can be followed.

Viewing and printing:
The concept search produces relevancy-ranked results as patent numbers and titles leading to the bibliographic details and an exemplary claim. There are then options to view the full text, to download it or to view the image of the patent (from IBM). The full text can optionally be delivered to an e-mail address.

Content ★★   Searching ★★   Viewing and printing ★★★ Help ★★

Inpadoc

National Informatics Centre Inpadoc – key facts

URL:	**http://pk2id.delhi.nic.in/sera.html**
Available from:	The Indian National Informatics Centre. Registration is required before use but no subscription is charged.
Produced by:	The European Patent Office. This database is also available free of charge from IBM (*see* page 17) and for a subscription through Questel-Orbit at **http://www.questel.orbit.com/**, Dialog at **http://www.dialogweb.com/** and STN at **http://stnweb.fiz-karlsruhe.de/** or **http://www.cas.org/stn.html**

Content:
Bibliographic data (no abstracts) from 1968 for about 80 countries. At the time of writing (June 2000) the latest data was from patents issued 6 months previously (but Inpadoc subscription databases and IBM Website are up-to-date).

Searching:
Two search masks are provided: Equivalent patent search and Bibliographic search. The Equivalent search allows the entry of a patent number and selection of a patent country.

The Bibliographic search allows database year ranges to be selected and for the search strategy to be entered in a single box. Classification symbols, patent numbers, publishing and priority country and dates must be entered exactly (Exact Search) as they appear in the record (i.e. no truncation) e.g. for the International Patent Classification enter ip = 'G11B 13/00'. Boolean operators 'AND', 'OR', 'AND NOT' can be used to link terms e.g. to specify only British patents pc = 'GB' AND ip = 'G11B 13/00'. Title words and inventors' and applicants' names must be entered as an inclusive search e.g. ap incl 'smith' or in incl 'dyson' for applicant or inventor name respectively. Adjacency operators and truncation are also possible with the inclusive search. Title words can be entered in the same way but this is not recommended as a method for subject searching as only brief information is given in the title and many languages are used. Access to this database is sometimes slow and use of Inpadoc on the IBM site is generally superior.

Viewing and printing:
The results of a search are presented as a single list of all the hits with complete bibliographic details.

Content ★★   Searching ★   Viewing and printing ★   Help ★

Community of Science

Community of Science – key facts

URL: http://www.cos.com

Produced by: Community of Science. Individual and corporate annual subscriptions.

Coverage:
Front page data of US patents from 1975.

Search:
There are four search entry screens. The main screen allows any text search terms

to be entered in the 'Full text' box or specific terms to be entered into specific field boxes (e.g. Abstract, Exemplary Claims). The different field boxes are linked with Boolean logic ('AND', 'OR', 'NOT'). The format used in the IPC field varies. The format of the US classification uses hyphens to separate parts of the classification e.g. 424-085-100. Right-hand truncation (*), phrase searching and proximity operators are available.

The Search by classification allows you to move down the hierarchy of the US patent classification schedules to select one or more relevant subclasses. The search is then carried out over a specified date range using the selected subclasses. It is not possible to search an index to the classification.

The other search screens allow the search to be limited to one particular country or state for the inventor or assignee (patent owner). Query tracking allows earlier searches to be revisited.

Viewing and printing:

A search generates a results list ranked by relevancy giving relevancy rating, patent number, title and assignee for the first 25 – 1000 hits. Clicking the patent numbers listed brings up the bibliographic data and claim including links to cited patents and a link to later citing patents. The front page data and an exemplary claim can be downloaded as a batch for selected patents.

Content *   Searching **   Viewing and printing **   Help *

1790.com

PatIntelligence – key facts

URL:	http://www.1790.com/
Produced by:	1790.com (formerly) Corporate Intelligence. Subscription service with monthly and other rates.

Coverage:
Full-text of US patents from 1945.

Search:
The full text and front page data can be searched using a simple entry screen.

Viewing and printing:
The P-Shoe Flip Searching feature allows browsing through front page information, drawings and the exemplary claim. Copies of patents can be requested as PDF files or sent by fax or post.

Chemical Patents Plus

Chemical Patents Plus

URL:	http://casweb.cas.org/chempatplus/
Produced by:	Chemical Abstracts Service. Subscription service providing searching and some display without charge.

Coverage:
Full-text of US patents from 1975 plus some material from 1971. All subject matter is covered but additional indexing is available for chemical patents.

Search:
The search screen allows searching in the 'Basic text and CAS indexing' or selected fields. Search terms are then entered in a box using Boolean logic as required. Stemming and other options can be set.

Viewing and printing:
A search produces a list of patent titles which can be selected for viewing of the abstract. Pages of selected patents can be viewed and printed. Additional information is provided on chemical structures.

Chapter 6.   Other Single Country Databases and Journals

Australia
http://www.ipaustralia.gov.au/services/S_srch.htm
Australian patents and patent applications filed since January 1979. Note that only a limited number of the data fields can be used for searches. PatIndex allows search using International Patent Classification marks. Special downloadable software required.

Brazil
http://www.inpi.gov.br
Patent applications and granted patents, text of current gazette Revista de patentes.

Bulgaria
http://www.online.bg/bpo/engl/issue.htm
Patent Abstracts of Bulgaria as English-language abstracts from May 1997 in monthly segments in PDF format.

Canada
http://Patents1.ic.gc.ca/intro-e.html
Titles, bibliographic information and images of patents and published applications from 1920 with abstracts and claims from 1978.

http://napoleon.ic.gc.ca/cipo/patgazarc.nsf/f_maincpor_e?Open Form
Canadian Patent Office Record (Canada's patent gazette) from April 1999 in PDF format.

Czech Republic
http://www.upv.cz/english/vestnik.html
Gazette from 2000. Part A is for inventions, with each issue in PDF format.

European Patent Office

http://www.european-patent-office.org/epo/pubs/
oj_index_e.htm

Official Journal of the European Patent Office in PDF format from January 1997.

Germany

http://www.patentblatt.de/eng/

DPMApatentblatt database of DE, EP and WO documents produced by
Bundesdruckerei. Free and subscription services.

Hungary

http://www.hpo.hu/English/

Hunpatéka database covers patents (including pending) and utility models from
1896. Hungarian granted patent documents in downloadable format from HU
210667 onwards in PDF format. Searchable English-language monthly Gazette
(from March 1996).

Italy

http://web.tin.it/fildata/indexen.htm

FILDATA. Published Italian patent and utility model applications filed after 1
January 1996 searchable by applicant and title. Brief details.

Japan

http://www2.ipdl.jpo-miti.go.jp/PA0/wHostCheck_e

Patents Abstracts of Japan (PAJ) English-language abstracts from 1993. This site
offers some status information and machine-translation of the full specification.
PAJ is also available on a number of other sites covering a greater time span (*see*
Esp@cenet page 10, IBM page 17, PATON page 21, and MicroPatent page 26).

http://patolis-e.japio.or.jp/

The PATOLIS database produced by JAPIO contains patents from 1955 and
utility models from 1960. Full status details. Now with a machine-translated
English-language service. Subscription only.

http://www.bunsan.japio.or.jp/

Bunsan service entirely in Japanese.

Patent Co-operation Treaty
http://www.wipo.org/eng/pct/gazette/weekissu.htm
Reproduction of each issue of the PCT Gazette in PDF format from April 1998.

Romania
http://bd.osim.ro/cgi-bin/invsearch
Romanian Patent Database from 1997. Each issue available either in a version requiring a Romanian character set or PDF version.

Russia
http://www.fips.ru/defen.htm
Patent abstracts of Russia. English abstracts from 1994. Also available at PATON (*see* page 21).

Spain
http://www.oepm.es/internet/bopi/bopi.htm
Last 4 weeks' gazettes (patents, utility models, trade marks) in PDF format.

Thailand
http://www1.ipic.moc.go.th/query.html
Thai Patent Database.

For European countries *see* also Esp@cenet on page 10.

Chapter 7.   Tracking Patents and Getting Copies

Patent status

The key stages in a patent's life may include: filing (in home country); filing abroad; publication of the application; withdrawal; grant and patent publication; publication of translation; opposition; amendment; revocation; renewal; lapsing; and expiry. Unless the patent application is withdrawn or refused the patent specification will be published and in some countries it will be published more than once. The usual convention is that at the first publication the patent document number is given a suffix A, the second publication, where it happens, B and so on. In searching for novelty the first publication is most important because it is earliest and discloses the most information but for determining the infringement position the last publication is most important. (For further details of the A and B codes go to the World Intellectual Property Organization Web page **http://www.wipo.org/eng/general/pcipi/standard/index.htm** and click on ST.16 Recommended standard code for the identification of different kinds of patent documents.)

If your aim is to search patents to check the 'state of the art' or to check the novelty of an invention then status of the patents found is not important as everything that has been published will need to be considered. For other situations, particularly for searching to see whether infringement of someone's patent is likely, then status is very important so as to know whether patents which have relevant subject matter are in force.

Each patent office will have an official register which tracks changes in the status of the patent. The changes in status are also recorded in an official gazette published periodically by the patent office concerned. In the case of British patents a known patent number (British or granted European which designates UK) or a known British patent application number can be searched at **http://webdb4.patent.gov.uk/patents/**. This search will show whether the patent application has been granted and whether it is still active as well as any assignments to a new proprietor. In the case of applications for British patents limited information is available within a few days of the application being filed and full information commences when the application is published. European patent information is on the British register as soon as a European Patent designating the UK is granted.

Before grant of a European patent and during any opposition procedure after grant the status information is held by the European Patent Office on its register. It is planned that the European Patent Register will be made available by the European Patent Office during 2000. It will be possible to search by a number of fields: Patent number, publication date, application number, filing date, applicant name, inventor name, representative name, opponent and classification (IPC). If there is more than one result from a search a list of patent publication numbers with the application number, applicant name and IPC is obtained. Clicking on any particular record produces the register information for that case. It is possible to view all the data which has to be kept in the register (according to Rule 92 of the European Patent Convention implementing regulations) or additional data or selected items, including either the current information or historical detail as well, each option being selected from a box near the head of the pages. References are sometimes made to articles, e.g. A96(2), within the European Patent Convention and the regulations (*see* page 43). Interpretation of this information can be quite complex and legal opinion should be sought if the outcome is important. To access this service go to **http://www.epoline.org/** or **http://www.european-patent-office.org/**. It is intended to link the register entries to an electronic file of the documents exchanged between the applicant, or the representative agent, and the patent office examiner (*see* later in this section).

There are several sources for US status information. Expired US patents, where the owner has failed to pay maintenance (renewal) fees, can be searched at **http://www.uspto.gov/expwd/expform.htm**. The Patent Application Information Retrieval database **http://pair.uspto.gov/** enables the File Contents History (actions taken by the US Patent and Trademark Office including issue of Correction Certificates) to be found for any US patent number or patent application number in the form N/nnnnnn, where N is the series number (which is 5 for patents applied for 1970-78, 6 for 1979-86, 7 for 1987-92, 8 for 1993-97 and 9 from 1998) and nnnnnn is the application number as printed on patent documents. Occasionally, patents are withdrawn just before grant and a patent number is allocated although the patent is never issued and these cases are listed at **http://www.uspto.gov/expwd/withdrwn.txt**. The CLAIMS/U.S. Patents Database (subscription service described above at page 28) also contains status information for US patents. Derwent have a similar file available through Questel.Orbit (*see* **http://www.derwent.com/prodserv/dwpi/patstatus.html**).

For Japanese patents some status information is available on Patents Abstracts of Japan (PAJ) on the Japanese Patent Office site at **http://www2.ipdl.jpo-miti.go.jp/PA0/wHostCheck_e**. At the end of some of the English-language abstracts are the dates of key actions in the JPO. Information is updated every two weeks. The Patolis subscription database is the primary source of information on Japanese patents and utility models and has recently become available in an English-language version on the Web. It is the fullest source of status information. (*See* page 34.)

The INPADOC legal status database, Patent Register Service (PRS), produced by the European Patent Office, is available via IBM (*see* page 17) and the same commercial hosts which offer the INPADOC bibliographic file (*see* page 29). PRS provides reasonably up-to-date information concerning the legal status of a patent or patent application that corresponds to what each country publishes in its own official gazette. A search performed in PRS for a given patent or application number yields a list in which each legal action is identified by a so called PRS-code (*see* **http://www.european-patent-office.org/inpadoc/ prs_description.htm**), followed by a short standardised text in English and the corresponding domestic language. Countries covered are AT, AU, BE, BR, CH, CL, DD, DE, DK, EP, ES, FI, FR, GB, HU, IE, IL, IT, LT, LU, MC, MD, NL, PH, PT, SE, US, WO.

In the case of European patents the complete file of correspondence between the European Patent Office and the applicant or representative for any particular case can be inspected after the patent application is published. It is planned that the files will become available on the Web as part of the 'epoline' service, which permits electronic filing of patent applications. File histories, or file wrappers as the correspondence about a patent application is known in the US, are normally obtained as paper files by paying a fee to the patent office concerned or from an independent organisation such as those listed as suppliers of patent copies below (*see* page 40).

Most patent databases will not record the current owner of a patent if it has changed since first publication of the specification. This means that searching for a company name may miss patents which were originally applied for by another organisation. For a known patent it is possible to use the methods described above to check ownership. If the owner of the patent licenses the patent rights to another party this will be recorded in the patent register if the law requires it but otherwise there may be no public record. There are some databases which record patents available for licence (*see* for example the various sites under Resources for inventors, page 46). The IBM Intellectual property Network (page 17) indicates patents which the owners have recorded with IBM as available for licence. It is sometimes said that any patent is potentially open to offers for licences so possibly use of a general patent database is a good starting point for finding patents available for licence.

Patent term extensions

Many countries now allow extensions to the 20 year term of patents for pharmaceuticals, veterinary drugs, plant protection products, medical devices etc. to compensate the owners for loss of effective patent term while the drug or other product is being tested for licensing by the regulatory authority. There are occasionally other grounds for extensions. In the UK extensions (Supplementary Protection Certificates or SPCs) are dealt with by the UK Patent Office and information will be given in the official register (*see* above) against individual patents.

In the case of extensions to US patents the US Food and Drug Administration (FDA) publishes in the Federal Register applications for extensions and if an extension is granted the United States Patent and Trademark Office puts the information on the USPTO site at **http://www.uspto.gov/web/offices/ pac/dapp/opla/term/**. The US Center for Drug Evaluation and Research, a unit within the FDA, publishes the Electronic Orange Book which lists current approved drug products by proprietary name, ingredient, application number and proprietor and the entries show the patent expiry date inclusive of any extensions at **http://www.fda.gov/cder/ob/default.htm**. Data on US extensions is also given in the Claims database (*see* patent status above).

The Inpadoc Patent Register Service contains details of SPCs for the countries covered (*see* above). Many pharmaceutical databases will also cover SPCs but detail on subject-based services is outside of the scope of this book.

Patent family information

To obtain the patent family for an invention, i.e. to locate all of the patent documents relating to a single invention (equivalents), you will need to search a database that covers all of the countries in which you are interested or possibly search several databases covering different countries. The most comprehensive databases in terms of country coverage are Esp@cenet, Derwent WPI (subscription), and Inpadoc. IBM, MicroPatent and GlobalPat also include family information. As noted above under most patent systems the patent specification is published twice and both documents will form part of the family but generally a family for any significant invention will, eventually at least, include members from different countries.

To retrieve the details of the patent family you will need to have to hand the patent number or the priority details (original application number and date) and to search for either of these. Sometimes an invention is applied for as a single patent in one country but split into two or more patents in the same or another country and in this case the relationship between the members of the 'extended family' will be complex. An Esp@cenet help screen provides some basic information on how families can be defined at **http://dips-2.dips.org/dips/ help/world/data3.htm** and the Patent Information User Group has details of how databases build family data at **http://www.piug.org/patfam.html**. The tracking of equivalent patents in the databases generally relies on the applicant for the patent claiming priority under the international Paris Convention which allows an application abroad to be made within 12 months of the original application at home while being treated as though the foreign applications were made on the same day as the original. In this case the applicant cites the priority details on the home country patent application which are then recorded against the new patent application. Sometimes foreign applications do not take advantage of the Convention but nevertheless still relate to the same invention. In this case these 'non-convention' applications have to be tracked manually. This can be done by searching in a database for patent applications by the same inventor but the tracking is provided alongside convention priorities as part of the Derwent WPI database.

Getting hold of copies

There are now several sites on the Web where patents specifications in their entirety can be viewed and printed without charge. These include Esp@cenet, the United States Patent and Trademark Office site and IBM Intellectual Property Network.

Esp@cenet covers a very large number of patent specifications from many countries including GB, EP, US and WO. The pages of the specifications may be viewed page by page by clicking on the appropriate buttons for 'Desc' (Description), 'Claims', 'Drawing', 'Next' (next page), 'S.R.' (Search report) etc. With Esp@cenet it is necessary to install Adobe Acrobat Reader to view and print the pages. Pages may be printed one by one within the Acrobat application. The Esp@cenet site gives details of how to download this software. During searching it is possible to add patents to the 'shopping basket' and then to send your list to one of the patent offices for dispatch of the copy but at the time of writing this feature had not been activated.

In the case of the United States Patent and Trademark Office site pages it is necessary to install a TIFF viewer. Details of getting this software are given on the United States Patent and Trademark Office site. The pages are viewed by searching and then clicking on the 'Images' button. The first page is displayed and the possibilities are given at any time to view the 'Front Page', 'Drawings', 'Specifications', or 'Claims', or to go to a particular page number or forward or back.

In the case of the IBM Intellectual Property Network site a search will provide bibliographic details and a thumbnail image of the front page. Clicking on this thumbnail displays the full front page and the remaining pages can be retrieved in one go by clicking on 'View Images'. You can then move through the downloaded pages. The pages (GIF files) need no special software for viewing but it is difficult to print a good copy of the original. As well as viewing the patents without charge you can alternatively pay for a higher quality copy of patents in high-resolution software formats or in hard copy. *See* page 17 for the patent specifications (images) available online on the IBM IPN site.

On any of these free services successive pages of the documents have to be printed individually, one at a time. As an alternative, it is possible to use Lattice software to download all pages of one or more patents automatically in one action from Esp@cenet, the United States Patent and Trademark Office site, IBM IPN or the Canadian Patent Office. This software is available without charge as shareware from Image Applications at **http://www.imageapps.co.uk/**. Registration of the shareware enables additional functions.

It is also now possible to order copies of patents over the Web from a number of other suppliers including the British Library's own Patent Express service. Patent Express **http://www.bl.uk/services/bsds/pxp/** allows online setting up of an account and online ordering. Copies are taken from the British Library's extensive collections (*see* the British Library holdings of patent specifications at **http://www.bl.uk/services/stb/collmenu.html**) and 98% of requests are satisfied from the in-house stock. Copies are currently delivered by post, fax, and courier.

Other suppliers can deliver electronic or paper copies. These include MicroPatent **http://www.micropat.com**, the United States Patent and Trademark Office (but not for electronic delivery) **http://www.uspto.gov/go/ptcs/**, IBM IPN **http://www.patents.ibm.com/home**, Optipat **http://www.optipat.com/**, Reedfax **http://www.reedfax.com/** and most of the services listed in Chapters 4 and 5. There are other services which can supply US and sometimes other country's patent documents (*see* the Patent Information User Group site at **http://www.piug.org/vendor.html** for a list).

Chapter 8.   Patent Law

UK

UK law

The current patent law in the United Kingdom is the Patents Act 1977. The text of this law and other relevant British legislation (particularly parts of The Patents, Designs and Copyright Act 1988) can be found along with commentary written for and by patent office examiners in the UK Patent Office's Manual of Patent Practice **http://www.patent.gov.uk/dpatents/mpp/intro.html**.

More recent general British statutes (from January 1996) can be found (with extensive extracts from many earlier statutes) at **http://www.hmso.gov.uk/ acts.htm**.

Statutory Instruments including the rules which implement the patents acts are available from 1997 onwards at **http://www.hmso.gov.uk/stat.htm**. The 1995 Patent Rules are at **http://www.jenkins-ip.com/patlaw/intro.htm**. A list of Statutory Instruments in force is given at **http://www.cipa.org.uk/notices/ statinst.htm**.

A growing archive of intellectual property law can be found at the World Intellectual Property Organization's site called CLEA, Collection of Laws for Electronic Access. It covers acts and rules in the UK and almost 40 countries worldwide, *see* **http://www.wipo.int/clea/**.

UK court decisions

Judgements about intellectual property cases in the UK may be made at the Patent Office, in the Patents County Court, the High Court (Patents Court), the Court of Appeal (Civil Division) or in the House of Lords. As a result of a case, the patent in dispute may be amended or revoked and the Patent Office register will reflect the outcome (*see* the section on status above).

The Patent Office site **http://www.patent.gov.uk/decisions/index.html** includes all decisions made by the Patent Office since the beginning of 1998. In addition, the Patent Office intend to add selected historical decisions in future.

The following databases on the Web cover not only intellectual property law cases but other areas of law as well. Not all cases are reported and not all reported cases are on the Web. High Court Decisions relating to intellectual property are beginning to be given in full on the official site at **http://www.courtservice.**

gov.uk/. It includes Practice Directions and a Court Diary. The court shorthand writers, Smith Bernal, also offer a similar database giving Court of Appeal cases from April 1996 at **http://www.smithbernal.com/**. House of Lords Judgements delivered since 14 November 1996 are available on the site **http://www.parliament.the-stationery-office.co.uk/pa/ld199697/ ldjudgmt/ldjudgmt.htm.**

European and International law

The text of the European Patent Convention and implementing legislation is available at **http://www.european-patent-office.org/legal/epc/index.html**. There is also a tool to combine and link information found in the European Patent Convention to the corresponding texts in the Guidelines for Examination at **http://www.european-patent-office.org/epc97/english/english/ index_fr.htm.**

European patents can be opposed within nine months of grant by filing an opposition with the European Patent Office. This may lead to a Decision from the EPO Boards of Appeal in the language of the proceedings (English, French or German). The texts of every decision despatched after 1 January 1995 are available at **http://www.european-patent-office.org/dg3/search_dg3.htm**.

The European Commission, which is the civil service of the European Union (EU), is a separate institution to the European Patent Office and it is the former that regulates the internal market of the EU countries. The European Commission Directorate General for the Internal Market operates a number of initiatives in the patent area and frames directives and regulations which the member countries have to adopt. Detail on these activities is given at **http:// europa.eu.int/comm/internal_market/en/intprop/index.htm**.

A French jurisprudence database is available, in French with an English-language version promised, at **http://ballot-schmit.com/jpfrance/pagepre.htm**.

The Paris Convention for the Protection of Industrial Property, which regulates treatment of applications for Intellectual Property Rights by foreign nationals within national patent and trade mark systems, and The Patent Co-operation Treaty and its regulations are given in the World Intellectual Property Organization's CLEA site **http://www.wipo.int/clea/**. The Agreement on Trade-Related Aspects of Intellectual Property Rights (TRIPs) is given at the World Trade Organization site at **http://www.wto.org/wto/intellec/1-ipcon.htm**. For a more practical guide to the application of these international laws follow the links from Chapter 2 on patents and patenting on page 4.

USA

The CLEA database also gives text of relevant US Federal laws. The US Code may also be searched at other sites, e.g. the Cornell Law School Legal Information Institute at **http://wwwsecure.law.cornell.edu/federal/**.

The opinions of the Federal Circuit since August 1995 (not just patent cases) are at the Emory University School of Law at **http://www.law.emory.edu/fedcircuit/**. The Litalert database from Derwent covers patent suits filed in US District Courts (*see* **http://www.derwent.com/prodserv/dwpi/litalert.html**). There are so many sites devoted to intellectual property law in the USA that a look at the portal sites which provide lists of links might be useful e.g. **http://www.bitlaw.com/index.html**, **http://www.ipmall.fplc.edu/pointbox/pointbox.htm** and **http://kuesterlaw.com/**. For more practical advice the Oppedahl & Larson Intellectual Property Law Web Server at **http://www.patents.com/** could be useful.

Some of the law firms listed in the following chapter also give details of law and case law.

Chapter 9.   News and General Resources

Organisations

Law firms

Chapter 2 has referred to patent agents or patent attorneys as a source of advice on patenting and patent protection. A useful source of links more generally is Piper's Worldwide listing of patent attorneys and agents compiled by New Zealand patent agents, Piper, which gives all patent agents by country, with e-mail addresses and Web links. This site is at **http://www.piperpat.co.nz/resource/world.html**. The Directory of Intellectual Property Law Firms published in association with The World Intellectual Property Network is a list of over 9,000 Intellectual Property law firms at **http://www.ip.lawnt.com/**.

Other law bodies relevant to patents include the following:

- The Chartered Institute of Patent Agents is the British association of patent attorneys. Site at **http://www.cipa.org.uk/**.

- American Intellectual Property Law Association site at **http://www.aipla.org/**.

- American Bar Association: Section of Intellectual Property Law at **http://www.abanet.org/intelprop/home.html**.

- FICPI, the Fédération Internationale des Conseils en Propiété Industrielle, is an international organisation whose membership consists solely of intellectual property professionals in private practice. It has members in 70 countries. Site at **http://www.ficpi.org/ficpi/**.

- The Licensing Executives Society International (LESI) is an association of national and regional societies, each composed of individuals with an interest in the transfer of technology, or licensing of intellectual property rights. Their website is at **http://lesi.org/**.

- The National Association of Patent Practitioners (NAPP) at **http://www.napp.org/** is an American, non-profit organisation for support of patent practitioners and those working in the field of patent law, its practice and technological advances.

Individual law firms are only listed in this book where they are known to have significant resources available on their Web pages which fall into categories covered.

Inventors' associations

- The British Institute of Patentees and Inventors at **http://www.invent. org.uk/** is a non-profit making association of over 1,000 members. It offers its members advice and guidance on all aspects of inventing from idea conception to innovation and development.

- The British Institute of Inventors is a voluntary, non-profit club, run by engineer inventors, aimed at sharing knowledge, experience and advice to maximise inventors' chances of earning money on their inventions. Its site is at **http://members.aol.com/mikinvent/index.html**.

- IFIA, the International Federation of Inventors' Associations is at **http:// www.invention-ifia.ch/**.

- The National Congress of Inventor Organizations (NCIO) is a US non-profit umbrella organisation offering education, training and support to inventor organisations. Its site is at **http://www.inventionconvention. com/ncio/**.

Resources for inventors

- The Eureka Club is a British site enabling inventions to be promoted and services advertised. Site is at **http://www.eureka-club.com/**.

- Innovate Now. This site managed by the UK Department of Trade and Industry's Innovation Unit has a knowledge base, a section on financing innovation, investigations into how highly innovative and successful organisations are managing people and a step-by-step guide to using Invention Promoters. Site at **http://www.innovation.gov.uk/**.

- The IPR Helpdesk is part of the European Commission's Innovation Programme. It focuses on assisting those given European Union funding for research and development but also provides useful information for others. Site is at **http://www.cordis.lu/ipr-helpdesk/en/home.html**.

- LISUN is a British site with advice for inventors at **http://www.lisun.co.uk/**.

- About.Com is a US inventors site with numerous links to histories of particular inventions. Site at **http://inventors.about.com/education/inventors/**.

- The US site of Brown, Pinnisi & Michaels, PC contains advice on its patents page about Invention Marketing companies. Site at **http://www.lightlink. com/bbm/index.html**.

- IFIS is a catalogue of offers of inventions from inventors or innovative companies who are directly or indirectly members of IFIA, the International

Association of Inventors Associations. Site is at **http://www.invention-ifia.ch/store.htm**.

- InventNet is a US site for inventors and includes help for inventors and details of inventions for sale. Site is at **http://www.inventnet.com/page1.html**.

- Lemelson-MIT Program's Invention Dimension is a US site for inventors. It includes an awards programme, inventor's handbook etc. Site is at **http://web.mit.edu/invent/**.

- The National Congress of Inventors Organizations is a US site that features free articles, information, resources, and an online magazine 'America's Inventor Online'. Its site is at **http://www.inventionconvention.com/ncio**.

- Michael Neustel's US National Inventor Fraud Center gives information about fraudulent activities of companies promoting inventions and lists inventor resources including groups, shows and websites; review of state statutes against fraud; victims' stories about experience with specific companies; information about how to recover funds spent on fraudulent patent services. Site is at **http://www.inventorfraud.com**.

- InventorEd's US site offers listing of known and alleged fraudulent invention promotion companies by name at **http://www.InventorEd.org/caution/**.

- An independent inventor resource at the official United States Patent and Trademark Office. Site at **http://www.uspto.gov/web/offices/com/iip/index.htm**.

Libraries and search organisations

Patent Depository libraries are often a good place to start searching. Many of them offer access for the public to patent services on the Internet (some without charge). They will also offer other resources and will have staff who are knowledgeable about patent searching. The UK Patents Information Network libraries are listed with the resources they hold at **http://www.bl.uk/services/stb/pinmenu.html**. European libraries in the PatLib network are listed at the European Patent Office site at **http://www.european-patent-office.org/patlib/index.htm**. The US Patent and Trademark Depository Libraries listing of US libraries is at **http://www.uspto.gov/web/offices/ac/ido/ptdl/index.html**.

Many organisations will conduct a search for you for a fee. The British Library has such a service, Patents Online, and further details are given at **http://www.bl.uk/services/stb/servmenu.html**. A good list of other searching organisations is given on the European Patent Office links page at **http://www.european-patent-office.org/online/index.htm**.

Policy research organisations

International Association for the Protection of Industrial Property claims to be The world's leading non-government organisation for research into, and formulation of policy for, the law relating to the protection of intellectual property. It is at **http://www.aippi.org/**.

The Intellectual Property Forum does not have a written constitution, but, in broad terms, it aims to raise awareness of the role and importance of intellectual property (IP) in the UK economy and improve the quality of debate about IP. Its site is at **http://info.sm.umist.ac.uk/eg/**.

The Max Planck Institute for Foreign and International Patent, Copyright and Competition Law in Munich undertakes comparative research in the field of national, European and international intellectual property law. Its site is at **http://www.intellecprop.mpg.de/Enhanced/English/Homepage.htm**.

Patent searchers associations

The Patent and Trade Mark Group (PATMG) is a special interest Group of the British Institute of Information Scientists. Their site is at **http://www.luna. co.uk/~patmg/**. The Group functions as a collective voice for members in dealing with national and international bodies and also holds patent information workshops, training courses on online retrieval and lectures covering various aspects of patent law.

A similar American group is the Patent Information User Group (PIUG) at **http://www.piug.org/**.

Both groups are associations of patent searchers and they participate jointly in an e-mail discussion group. Members and non-members can submit information and questions on topics related to patent searching. Details of joining the list are given on the PIUG site.

Pressure Groups

The Intellectual Property Owners Association represents the interests of American owners of intellectual property at **http://www.ipo.org/**.

Alliance for American Innovation is a Washington presence for individuals and organisations in the US which are interested in the entrepreneurial process, and the laws that provide its basis. The Alliance also serves as a depository of information on issues, particularly on intellectual property. Site at **http://www.Alliance-DC. org/**.

Newsletters and journals

The following is a selection of some of the most useful sites reporting current and recent intellectual property cases going through the courts and other news.

- Text of Patent Co-operation Treaty monthly newsletter from the World Intellectual Property Organization. Site at **http://www.wipo.org/ eng/pct/newslett/**.

- Newsletters and special information bulletins covering international news from intellectual property law firm, Ladas & Parry. Site at **http://www. ladas.com/ladasnews.html**.

- Derwent Patent news consisting of selected brief stories on recent news (mainly court cases) from Reuters. Site at **http://www.derwent.com/ news/articles/**.

- Berkeley technology law journal is a student-run publication of the Boalt Hall School of Law, University of California at Berkeley. It covers emerging issues of law in the areas of intellectual property and biotechnology. Site at **http://www.law.berkeley.edu/journals/btlj/**.

- Chicago-Kent journal of intellectual property. Site at **http://www.kentlaw. edu/student_orgs/jip/index.html**.

- Journal of intellectual property law from the University of Georgia, USA. Site at **http://www.lawsch.uga.edu/~jipl/index.html**.

- Harvard journal of law and technology. Site at **http://jolt.law.harvard.edu/**.

- Intellectual property and technology Law review from the University of Pittsburgh School of Law. Site at **http://www.pitt.edu/~stls/IPTLRev/ IPTLRev.htm**.

- Intellectual property today. Content is aimed at attorneys, patent agents and executives. Site at **http://www.lawworks-iptoday.com/**.

- IP Worldwide: US magazine of law and policy for high technology. Site at **http://ipmag.com**.

- ipFrontline. A monthly online intellectual property newsletter from US-based Manning and Napier Information Services. Site at **http://www.ip.com/ ipfrontline/index.html**.

- IPO daily news. US news from the Intellectual Property Owners Association. **http://www.ipo.org/DailyNews.htm**.

- Marquette intellectual property law review. Journal from the Marquette University Law School provides a forum for scholarly discussion of issues affecting American intellectual property law attorneys. Site at **http://www.mu.edu/law/ipwebpage/iplawrev.html**.

- PTO pulse and PTO today. US Patent and Trademark Office newsletters on its own activities. Sites at **http://www.uspto.gov/go/opa/pulse/** and **http://www.uspto.gov/web/offices/ac/ahrpa/opa/ptotoday/**.

- Texas intellectual property law journal (abstracts). Site at **http://www.utexas.edu/law/journals/tiplj/index.htm**.

Newsgroups

Your Internet Service Provider, aside from providing access to the Web, usually gives you access to newsgroups or discussion groups. By opening the discussion group server it is possible to list groups that are available and then to view the newsgroup or to subscribe. If you are subscribed opening the newsgroup server will update the messages. There are a number of groups on topics related to patents on which anyone can post messages, questions and answers. The most useful are: **news:alt.inventors** and **news:misc.int-property** which contain mainly US postings. You can look at the postings on Web services such as Deja.com at **http://w.deja.com/home_bg.shtml** or Liszt's Usenet Newsgroups Directory at **http://www.liszt.com/news/**.

There are also a number of discussion lists which you need to join to see the messages and which work by means of broadcasting of e-mail messages. The PIUG/PATMG list for patent searchers is mentioned on page 48. Another is the UK-based IPR-Science which can be joined by sending an e-mail containing the text 'join IPR-Science Your Name' to **mailto:mailbase@mailbase.ac.uk**. A US-based list is the Internet Patent News Service which circulates regular bulletins about US patent law and examination and other topics. To join the latter send an e-mail to **mailto:patents@world.std.com** and put 'help' in the subject line. The European Patent Office has a list for information on developments in and around European Patent Office products and services. It also allows list users to communicate with other users on the list. Further information is at **http://www.european-patent-office.org/mail.htm**. Intprop-l is a list addressing intellectual property, including patent law in Europe and further information on it and other lists can be obtained from **http://www.topica.com/lists/intprop-l**.

A listing on the Web of useful lists and groups for inventors is given at **http://inventors.tqn.com/education/inventors/msub7.htm#newsgroups**.

Statistics and patent analysis

Patent offices sites listed in Appendix 2 often give useful statistical information on their own activities. Generally the printed annual reports of the patent offices provide detail of the number of applications and grants made during the course of the year and this data is sometimes reflected in the patent office websites. Some of this information has been gathered together by the World Intellectual Property Organization and put on their site at **http://www.wipo.org/eng/general/ pcipi/stat-new/index.htm**. At present 1994–98 statistics for patents, trade marks, designs and utility models etc. are available on either Microsoft Excel or PDF formats. Older information is currently only available in printed format.

Of course, many of the search databases mentioned in Chapters 4, 5 and 6 can be used to find basic statistical information about numbers of patents in different categories, particularly by date or country of origin. See in particular GlobalPat (page 21) where there is a specific facility for tabular representation of results. They are less useful in producing data organised by applicant company because of the inconsistent way the names of the patent applicants are recorded making it more difficult to gather together a complete set of data for any applicant. Software is available to organise the results of these kinds of searches. BizInt Smart Charts for Patents is software which allows you to create tabular reports or charts from patents databases by importing your search results from STN or Questel.Orbit. You can create combined reports from the Derwent World Patents Index and IFI CLAIMS site at **http://www.bizcharts.com/sc4pats/**.

CHI Research is a US company that organises US patent and other data for citation research. Their Tech-Line database includes: patent information from the last ten years, broken down annually; indicators of technological strength; data on over 1000 of the top companies, research institutes and government agencies; and information divided into 26 industry groups and 30 technology areas. Site is at **http://www.chiresearch.com**.

IBM, as well as offering the Intellectual Property Network site (*see* page 17), offers a subscription site IPN for Business which offers enhanced searching and security over the free site. It also offers data analysis and visualisation tools.

IFI Claims produces a monthly and annual report called the Patent Intelligence & Technology Report. It provides information concerning the ownership and subject distribution of U.S. patents. As a special feature, the Report includes a six year analysis of the patent activities, by subject area, for each major and institutional assignee. Sample data available at **http://www.ificlaims.com/pit.htm**.

Manning & Napier Information Services (*see* also page 29) provides a subscription patent data mining services on the Web. The MapIT tool searches United States, EP and Patent Co-operation Treaty data using a natural language search system. The data set can then be analysed by data mining techniques to produce graphical output and clustering (categorisation) of the results. Site is at **http://www.mnis.net/**.

Mogee Research & Analysis prepares custom technology assessment and competitor intelligence reports based on the latest patent data from 40 countries, including the United States, Japan, and European nations. It also offers a suite of patent citation analyses designed to support patent licensing, patent portfolio management and R&D management. Site is at **http://www.mogee.com/**.

For further information on 'Software tools for analyzing patents' *see* the PIUG site at **http://www.piug.org/pattools.html**. See also Aurigin at **http://www. aurigin.com/**; Mapout at **http://www.mapout.se/**; Semoi at **http://www1. semio.com/** and Themescape at **http://www.cartia.com/**.

An extensive list of Internet resources on the topic of costs and the economics of patent acquisition, litigation, licensing (particularly in the US) is given at **http://www.bustpatents.com/economic.htm**.

Appendix 1. Glossary of Terms Used

Adjacency Operator   A search operator which allows records to be found where terms are present and are within a specified number of words of each other or within a single sentence or paragraph. (Operators are e.g. 'ADJ', 'NEAR' or 'PARAGRAPH'.)

AND   A Boolean operator which requires all specified terms to appear in a record.

ANDNOT   A Boolean operator (sometimes specified as 'NOT') which requires a first term to be present and a second term to be absent in a record.

Assignee   The person or organisation which owns, or has acquired, the rights to a patent.

Bibliographic information   Data concerned with the publication of a patent document. Includes publication number and date, application number and date, priority details, names of the inventors and applicant. Data usually found on the front page of a patent specification.

Boolean logic   Named after nineteenth-century mathematician George Boole. Boolean logic is a form of algebra in which all values are reduced to either TRUE or FALSE. It provides a way to combine search terms using operators such as 'AND', 'OR', 'AND NOT'.

Claim   The definition of the monopoly that the patent protects.

ECLA   European Classification, administered by the European Patent Office.

Equivalent patent   A different specification describing the same invention as the known document.

European Patent   A patent granted under the European Patent Convention, a treaty covering many European Countries

Family   The group of specifications published by the same or different patent offices for the same invention.

Full text	The complete text of a patent specification including the description and claims which is generally able to be searched
GIF	Graphics Interchange Format, an image file format
HTTP	HyperText Transfer Protocol
IPC	International Patent Classification, administered by the World Intellectual Property Organization.
NOT	A Boolean operator (sometimes specified as 'ANDNOT') which requires a first specified term to be present and a second specified term to be absent in a record.
OR	Boolean operator which requires either of two specified terms to be present in a record.
PDF	Portable Document Format. Adobe's proprietary format which produces files that can be viewed, annotated, and printed on any computer.
Priority	Claim to a patent based on an earlier application for a patent for the same invention (in a different or the same country).
Proximity searching	A search which allows records to be found where terms are present and are within a specified number of words of each other or within a single sentence or paragraph. (Uses operators e.g. 'ADJ' or 'NEAR'.)
Specification	The document containing the description of an invention, drawings and claims drawn up to support an application for a patent.
TIFF	Tagged Image File Format. A graphics file format frequently used for facsimile pages of a patent document. There are many variations on the format.
URL	Uniform Resource Locator, the address of a page on the Internet.
Utility model	A kind of patent available in some countries which involves a simpler inventive step and offers a shorter patent term than a regular patent.

XOR   Boolean operator which requires either of two specified terms to be present in a record but not both.

The IPR Help Desk had a useful glossary of patent searching terms at **http://www.ipr–helpdesk.org/mm/esptut/gloss/gloss.htm**.

Appendix 2. Patent Offices, their Country Codes and Web addresses

Patent Office	Code*	Web address (url)
Argentina	AR	http://www.mecon.gov.ar/inpi/default1.htm
Australia	AU	http://www.ipaustralia.gov.au/
Austria	AT	http://www.patent.bmwa.gv.at/
Belgium	BE	http://mineco.fgov.be
Bosnia and Herzegovina	BA	http://www.bih.net.ba/~zsmp/osn_pod_e.htm
Brazil	BR	http://www.inpi.gov.br/
Bulgaria	BG	http://www.online.bg/bpo/engl/Mainm.htm
Canada	CA	http://cipo.gc.ca/
China	CN	http://www.cpo.cn.net
Croatia	HR	http://jagor.srce.hr/patent/Novi/eng/index.html
Cuba	CU	http://www2.ceniai.inf.cu/OCPI/
Czech Republic	CZ	http://www.upv.cz/english/
Denmark	DK	http://www.dkpto.dk/english/start.htm
Eurasian Patent Organization	EA	http://www.eapo.org/english/index.html
European Patent Office	EP	http://www.european-patent-office.org
Finland	FI	http://www.prh.fi/
France	FR	http://www.inpi.fr
Georgia	GE	http://www.global-erty.net/saqpatenti
Germany	DE	http://www.deutsches-patentamt.de
Greece	GR	http://www.obi.gr/

*For a full list of codes *see* World Intellectual Property Organization Standard ST.3, Two-Letter Codes for the Representation of States, Other Entities and Organizations at http://www.wipo.org/eng/general/pcipi/standard/index.htm

Hong Kong	HK	http://www.info.gov.hk/ipd/
Hungary	HU	http://www.hpo.hu/English
Iceland	IS	http://www.els.stjr.is/
Ireland	IE	http://www.european-patent-office.org/ie/index.htm
Italy	IT	http://www.european-patent-office.org/it/
Japan	JP	http://www.jpo-miti.go.jp/
Korea	KR	http://www.kipo.go.kr/ehtml/eIndex.html
Lithuania	LT	http://www.is.lt/vpb/engl
Luxembourg	LU	http://www.etat.lu/EC/
Macedonia	MK	http://www.ippo.gov.mk
Malaysia	MY	http://kpdnhq.gov.my/ip/
Mexico	MX	http://www.impi.gob.mx/
Moldova	MD	http://www.agepi.md/
Monaco	MC	http://www.european-patent-office.org/patlib/country/monaco/
Netherlands	NL	http://www.bie.nl/engels/index.htm
New Zealand	NZ	http://www.iponz.govt.nz
Peru	PE	http://www.indecopi.gob.pe/
Philippines	PH	http://www.dti.gov.ph/bpttt/
Poland	PL	http://up.ci.uw.edu.pl/
Portugal	PT	http://www.inpi.pt
Romania	RO	http://www.osim.ro
Russia	RU	http://www.rupto.ru
Singapore	SG	http://www.gov.sg/minlaw/ipos/
Slovakia	SK	http://www.indprop.gov.sk/english/a_uvod.html
Slovenia	SI	http://www.sipo.mzt.si/GLAVAGB.htm
Spain	ES	http://www.oepm.es

Sweden	SE	http://www.prv.se/english/
Switzerland	CH	http://www.ige.ch/
Thailand	TH	http://www.dbe.moc.go.th/DIP/eng/index.html
Turkey	TR	http://www.turkpatent.gov.tr/english/tpi.htm
United Kingdom	GB	http://www.patent.gov.uk/
United States	US	http://www.uspto.gov/
Vietnam	VN	http://www.fpt.vn/adv/noip/
World Intellectual Property Organization	WO	http://www.wipo.org/eng/main.htm

Appendix 3. Coverage of the Esp@cenet Database

Country	Code	Abstracts	Images	Bibliographic Data
African Intellectual Property Organisation	OA	no	all	1966
African Regional Industrial Property Organisation	AP	no	all	all
Argentina	AR	no	no	1973
Australia	AU	no	no	1973
Austria	AT	no	1920	1975
Belgium	BE	no	1920	1964
Brazil	BR	no	no	1973
Bulgaria	BG	no	no	1973
Canada	CA	no	no	1970
China	CN	yes	no	1985
Croatia	HR	no	no	1994
Cuba	CU	no	no	1974
Cyprus	CY	no	no	1975
Czech Republic	CZ	no	no	1993
Czechoslovakia	CS	no	no	1973
Denmark	DK	no	1920	1968
Egypt	EG	no	no	1976
Eurasian Patent Office	EA	no	no	1996
European Patent Office	AP	yes	all	1978
Finland	FI	no	1920	1968
France	FR	yes	1920	1968
German Democratic Republic	DD	no	yes	1973

Germany	DE	yes	1920	1967
Greece	GR	no	no	1977
Hong Kong	HK	no	no	1976
Hungary	HU	no	no	1994
India	IN	no	no	1975
Ireland	IE	no	1996	1973
Israel	IL	no	no	1968
Italy	IT	no	1978	1973
Japan	JP	yes	1980	1973
Kenya	KE	no	no	1975
Korea, Republic of	KR	no	no	1978
Latvia	LV	no	no	1994
Lithuania	LT	no	no	1994
Luxembourg	LU	no	1945	1960
Malawi	MW	no	no	1973
Mexico	MX	no	no	1981
Moldova, Republic of	MD	no	no	1994
Monaco	MC	no	all	1975
Mongolia	MN	no	no	1972
Netherlands	NL	no	all	1964
New Zealand	NZ	no	no	1979
Norway	NO	no	no	1968
Philippines	PH	no	no	1975
Poland	PL	no	no	1973
Portugal	PT	no	1980	1976
Romania	RO	no	no	1973
Russian Federation	RU/SU	no	no	1972
Slovakia	SK	no	no	1993

Slovenia	SI	no	no	1992
South Africa	ZA	no	no	1971
Spain	ES	no	1968	1968
Sweden	SE	no	1918	1931
Switzerland	CH	yes	1920	1969
Turkey	TR	no	no	1973
United Kingdom	GB	yes	1920	1969
United States of America	US	no	1920	1968
Vietnam	VN	no	no	1984
World Intellectual Property Organization	WO	yes	all	1978
Yugoslavia	YU	no	no	1973
Zambia	ZM	no	no	1968
Zimbabwe	ZW	no	no	1980

Note:

- Abstracts shows presence or starting date of searchable and displayable abstract text.
- Images shows presence or starting date of viewable drawings etc. from the patent specification.
- Bibliographic data indicates the start date of information for that country.

Appendix 4. Bibliography

Principally covering patents in the UK

van Dulken, Stephen. *Introduction to patents information.* 3rd ed. London: British Library, 1998.

Reid, Brian C. *A practical guide to patent law.* 3rd ed. Sweet & Maxwell: London, 1999.

The inventor's guide: how to profit from your idea. Edited by the British Library Patents Information Team. Gower: London, 1997.

Principally covering patents in the US

Bryant, Joy L. *Protecting your ideas – the inventor's guide to patents.* Academic Press: San Diego and London, c1999.

Burge, David A. *Patent and trademark tactics and practice.* 3rd ed. John Wiley: New York and Chichester, c1999.

Durham, Alan L. *Patent law essentials – a concise guide.* Quorum: Westport, Conn. and London, 1999.

Sharpe, Charles C. *Patent, trademark, and copyright searching on the Internet.* McFarland, Jefferson: N.C. and London, 2000.

The Patent Information User Group have a bibliography on searching at **http://www.piug.org/patbib.html**. For further books on patents search the British Library catalogue at **http://opac97.bl.uk/**. For patent books search in the Science, Technology and Business (1975-) collection.

Information to help make you a genius

Thomas Edison said "Genius is one percent inspiration and ninety-nine percent perspiration". We can certainly help you reduce the sweat and toil involved in turning your ideas into something more. Who knows, our wealth of knowledge might even give you inspiration.

If you have an idea for an innovation you know that taking it further can be hard work. You need to check whether your idea is new and whether it has potential. That is where the British Library can help. We handle over 8 million requests for information each year - information that can make all the difference.

Information

We have extensive resources. These include 4 million reports, 271,000 journals, 44 million patents, as well as books, conference proceedings, theses, market research reports, electronic sources and access to information on the Internet. Our staff will help you locate the most appropriate sources.

Patent specifications are an important source of current technology giving detailed descriptions and drawings. The national collections of patents from 38 countries is held at our London site. Neglect patents as a source and you may find yourself reinventing the wheel.

Our **Business Information** literature collection is the most comprehensive in the UK. It includes market research reports and journals, directories, company annual reports, trade and business journals, house journals, trade literature and CD-ROM services. We cover the manufacturing, wholesale trading, retailing and distribution aspects of major industries, financial services, energy, environment, transport, and food and drink service sectors.

Our **Science, Technology and Medicine** literature collections cover life sciences and technologies, physical sciences and technologies, engineering, geology, meteorology, astronomy, mathematics, UK and foreign publications, British standards, and social science material, including education, law and theoretical management.

The Reading Rooms

You need a reader's pass to use the reading rooms on site. These are issued without charge to people who need to see material in the Library's collections that is not readily available elsewhere. To apply you need to complete an application form available from the Reader Admissions Office.

A Choice of Services

Basic requests are free. More complex queries are handled by one of our specialist research services. They can provide current awareness services, in-depth patents and subject searches; company, market or product profiles; names and addresses for direct mail; as well as copies of patents, journal articles, conference papers and other material.

Training and Publishing

We run a year-round programme of training workshops for information seekers at all levels. We also publish our own list of titles including: *Introduction to patents information*, 3rd edition.

Further Information

Please contact Marketing:
Tel: 020 7412 7473
Fax: 020 7412 7947
Email: stb-marketing@bl.uk
Web: http://www.bl.uk/services/stb/

Inventing the 20th Century:
100 Inventions that Shaped the World

By Stephen Van Dulken

Imagine your average day without television, vacuum cleaners, photocopiers and your personal stereo. All of these devices were invented within the last 100 years and have since transformed our daily lives.

Drawing on the British Library's vast and comprehensive collection of patents *Inventing the 20th century* is a handsomely illustrated book recounting the history of 100 of the most significant inventions of the 20th century, decade by decade. By combining a brief history of each patent with a copy of the original patent application illustration, *Inventing the 20th century* reveals the ways in which many of the most basic aspects of our material existence have been revolutionised through specific objects.

From the parking meter to the Slinky toy, from genetic fingerprinting to the lava-lamp, from the ballpoint pen to the fuel cell, *Inventing the 20th century* is an informative, illuminating window onto the technology of the last century.

PUBLICATION September 2000
246 pages, 100 b/w ills., 234x56mm, cloth
ISBN 0 7123 0866 0
£16.95 (Turpin Distribution Services Ltd)
ISBN 0 8147 8808 4
North and South America: $26.95 (Published in the USA by New York University Press, 883 Broadway, New York, NY 10003-4182. Tel: 212 998 2575, Fax: 212 995 3833, Email: nyupress.feedback@nyu.edu

How to Find Information: Genetically Modified Foods

By Rupert Lee

This new title will be of use to any non-specialist who needs to be well-informed on this hottest of topics. Written in jargon-free language, this guide points readers to the authoritative sources. Business people who need to keep abreast of developments, journalists, farmers, students, or any lay people concerned over the issues involved, will all find it a handy guide to keep on their desks.

Chapters cover the science of GM technology, sources of business and market information, government and regulatory information, public opinion, pressure groups and ethical debates. There is also a chapter on how best to use public libraries as information sources.

Important sites on the Internet are described, along with other, non-electronic methods of accessing the same information. Worked examples are given of how to track down such information as recent patents, the sites of field trials of GM crops, and what research projects the government is supporting. Dr Lee works in the British Library Science and Technology Information Service.

PUBLICATION June 2000
39 pages, 210x146mm, paper
ISBN 0 7123 0863 6
£9.95 (Turpin Distribution Services Ltd)
North America: $19.95 (University of Toronto Press)

Introduction to Patents Information

Edited by Stephen van Dulken, 3rd edition

Introduction to patents information is a practical step-by-step guide to searching for UK and overseas patent information.

Topics covered include:

- official printed data sources
- online and CD-ROM databases
- patent classification
- patent legislation

The guide covers patent searching worldwide but with particular emphasis on the UK and the rest of Europe, Japan and the USA. Beginners will find it gives them a complete introduction to patents searching, whilst more experienced searchers will find the text a useful refresher.

'It is a valuable reference source for anyone who needs to search for patents on technology.'
New Scientist, about the 2nd edition.

'If you can think of a better way of introducing readers to patents than this, then you had better patent it quickly.'
Reference Reviews.

PUBLICATION 1998

127 pages, 297×210mm, paper
ISBN 0 7123 0838 5
£32.00 (Turpin Distribution Services Ltd)
North America: $69.95 (University of Toronto Press)

Rooms near Chancery Lane

By John Hewish

It is fitting that this book has been published now as 25 Southampton Buildings near Chancery Lane, London, the home of the Patent Office and the Patent Office Library for the best part of 150 years, is their home no longer.

The book weaves a tale of considerable achievements under the Commissioners but at the same time reveals some extraordinary goings-on. At times eccentric and bizarre, like some of the inventions that were patented, the management of the Patent Office mixed private business and public service. Financial irregularities, nepotism and conflict between the two senior officials led to Government enquiry and censure involving the Lord Chancellor and other prominent figures. In all it shows the colourful history of a public office in Victorian Britain.

This book represents many years of diligent, rigorous and fruitful research by the author. It provides a fitting testimony to the Patent Office and Patent Office Library as catalysts of innovation at the time that these institutions adapt to the next millennium in rooms removed from Chancery Lane.

PUBLICATION April 2000

173 pages, 11 b/w ills., 234x156mm, cloth
ISBN 0 7123 0853 9
£35.00 (Turpin Distribution Services Ltd)
North America: $45.00 (University of Toronto Press)

British Patents of Invention, 1617-1977: A Guide for Researchers

By Stephen van Dulken

This unique guide, written by an expert in the British Library Patent Information Service, explains how researchers can use patents as a source of historical information. Covering the British patents system from 1617 until the 1977 Patents Act, the guide is an invaluable resource for anyone researching the history of science and technology or looking for information on the people behind the inventions.

Sections include:

- the historical background of the patent system
- patenting procedure
- people in the patent system
- the patent specifications
- searching for patents information

PUBLICATION 1999

211 pages, 297x210mm, paper
ISBN 0 7123 0817 2
£39.00 (Turpin Distribution Services Ltd)
North America: $69.95 (University of Toronto Press)

Orders to: Turpin Distribution Services Ltd, Blackhorse Road, Letchworth, Herts SG6 1HN, UK. Tel: 01462 672555, Fax: 01462 480947, Email: turpin@rsc.org

Orders in North America to: University of Toronto Press, 5201 Dufferin Street, Downsview, Ontario, M3H 5T8, Canada. Tel: 416 667 7791, Fax: 416 667 7832, Email: utbooks@utpress.utoronto.ca